MW00699504

Merlot & Brussels Sprouts

Merlot & Brussels Sprouts

Fundamentals of Pairing Wine with Plant-Based Foods

• • • • • •

Mandy Nash

Cover design by Brianne Fortier
Printed in the U.S.A
ISBN: 9781717703613

To the lover of food and wine

CONTENTS

Merlot & Brussels Sprouts

INTRODUCTION

Pick up any wine book on the market or go online and type "*What pairs well with Merlot*?" into the search engine and I guarantee you'll be met with a plethora of meat-based recipes that include steak, lamb, pork loins, and veal. Perhaps, you'll come across a recipe for spaghetti marinara... (as if that's original).

Not only are these meat-based search results frustrating for someone like me who's mostly vegan, but what about the other vegetarians? There are 7.5 million self-identified vegetarians in the United States alone. The overwhelming absence of vegetarian food and wine pairings was what motivated me to write this book.

I included *plant-based* in the title because as a certified nutrition coach and personal trainer, I believe in trying to eat a diet that's full of whole grains, lots of vegetables, nuts, seeds and legumes, with little to no dairy or meat products.

I was also strongly motivated to write a book that included everything you never thought you'd need to know about wine and the industry. And because of my health background, I had to write a chapter addressing the hype around wine being healthy. I truly hope you enjoy the book!

CHAPTER 1

• • • • • •

THE WINE TASTING EXPERIENCE

My experience as a wine educator was short but invaluable. I learned more than I ever could've imagined simply by being behind the counter and serving wine to customers. I quickly learned how to taste and describe wine, as well as how to sell it. As I collectively thought about all the diverse types of people who sat at my wine bar, it was clear to me that about half of my customers knew exactly what to expect at a wine tasting, while the other half had no idea. I really enjoyed the process of teaching people how to drink wine and creating what I like to call *the wine tasting experience*.

It Begins at Home....

Somebody has to decide where to go wine tasting, so let's assume that person is you. First, I recommend choosing no more than eight people at a time to go wine tasting, to make it easier for the winery to accommodate your group.

Second, choose friends/people you would want to go drinking with. If you have any friends who work in the wine industry, definitely invite them! Most wineries offer discounts for people that work within the wine industry, as well as complimentary tastings for friends of wine club members.

Choosing which wineries to visit can be a complicated task, especially when you're trying to accommodate the tastes and preferences of everyone in the group. Again, the smaller the group, the easier it is to plan.

I recommend picking four wineries to visit but only actually going to three. The fourth winery is your back up plan if you don't like the vibe of your first three choices.

I also suggest that you invite someone who doesn't drink wine to be the designated driver. DO NOT assume that you or anyone in your group that's been drinking, will be okay to drive. Buzzed driving is drunk driving, and we all want to be safe out there. So, plan ahead. There are plenty of other ways to get around, such as choosing wineries close enough to walk to, splitting the cost of a limo or calling a taxi, Lyft, or Uber... you get the idea.

I recommend carpooling, and either meeting everyone for breakfast before 11 a.m. or suggesting that people eat something before they go. Most wineries are open by 11 a.m. and you definitely want to have food in your system before you start drinking. I like to meet up with my friends for a light breakfast and start tasting shortly after the wineries open.

There are several benefits to being at a winery when it opens. First, the sooner you start tasting, the more time you have in the day to relax at the winery and possibly beat the crowds.

Second, being finished with your wine-tasting adventures by late afternoon, gives you ample time to drive home for dinner and beat rush hour traffic.

You can choose whether or not you and your group want to have lunch in between wineries or snack while you go, but don't assume wineries will offer crackers or breadsticks with their tastings, because most do not. I always bring snacks and stash them in my car for the breaks between wineries.

I also suggest spacing out your wine tastings. Take your time at each winery by walking the grounds, shopping, or hanging out at a café. You want to enjoy the experience of each winery and give your body time to digest the alcohol.

Proper etiquette while visiting wineries will greatly contribute to your wine tasting experience. And, it begins with what to wear.

Proper Attire

Have you ever wondered about the proper attire for wine tasting? Maybe you don't care, but you really should. And it's different for guys than girls.

Ladies: Most of us have a pretty good sense for occasions that require looking nice, right? Well, wine tasting is certainly one of those occasions! In the summer, it's appropriate to wear sleeveless tops, shorts (if they are khaki or otherwise not cut-off denim), and light flowy dresses are always a winner.

Wine tasting is a classy event, so I don't recommend showing up to wineries in a baseball cap and swimsuit top.

Cooler weather opens up a lot more options. Sweaters, leggings, boots, nice jackets, nice pants, and stylish beanies, are all accepted, and are pretty easy to put together. Fitted jeans and a dressy top can also work, but torn jeans and a T-shirt? Not so much.

And as much as this might seem obvious, avoid the nightclub look. You know what I mean-- the overly made-up face, tight leathers and sparkling one-strap zebra top? That is indeed not the attire for a classy activity like wine tasting. Also, I definitely recommend wearing comfortable shoes, as some wine bars are standing room only.

Gentlemen: You might think you have it easier than us ladies, but in actuality, women get away with a lot more. We get to wear things like tank tops and open-toe shoes, while men are advised against wearing sleeveless tops and flip-flops to wine tastings. And maybe it isn't *fair*, but do you really want to see another man's armpit hair or toe nails during your wine and cheese pairing? I'm just saying, assume the worse and save the tank for a day at the river. ☺

If it's a warm summer day, I suggest wearing khaki or solid-colored shorts, a plain crew or V-neck T-shirt, and nice closed-toe shoes. Cooler weather opens up a lot more options for men, as well. A simple solid colored T-shirt or sweater and nice jeans is perfect. Nice jackets are always welcome, and suits can work if you're doing the business-casual look but leave the tuxedo at home.

The Wine Bar

I highly recommend making a reservation for wine tasting if you're bringing a group of six or more people.

Generally, wineries can accommodate small groups of three to four people during the weekdays without a reservation, but I would definitely call ahead.

Most wineries offer two to three different tasting menus, at varying costs. I recommend choosing a tasting menu that includes wines you have never tasted before. It's totally okay to split a tasting (which my husband and I do all the time).

Once the wine is poured into your glass, follow these five steps…

The FIVE S's

1. **SWIRL** the wine around in your glass.
2. **SMELL** the aromatic molecules which were just released by swirling the wine.
3. **SEE** what the wine looks like in your glass. Is it translucent? Inky black? A salmon pink color? Does the wine stick to the glass before streaking down the side?
4. **SIP** the wine.
5. **SAVOR** the taste! Really pay attention to the body of the wine (in terms of weight, fullness, and texture). *Is the wine thick? Light? Acidic? Sweet? Does the wine linger at the back of your throat? Maybe your mouth feels dry or you get a burning sensation from the alcohol through your nose.*

I highly encourage you to gather as much information as you can about the wine you are tasting. By paying attention to the aspects of wine that you do or don't like, you will be able to determine your favorite kinds of wine.

So, what happens when you don't like one of the wines that's poured for you during a wine tasting? Well, if you're sharing a tasting, just make your partner drink it.

Otherwise, it's perfectly okay to dump the wine into a spittoon or bucket, which should be sitting on the wine bar. If there isn't a dumping bucket available, kindly let the tasting attendant know that you are finished with the wine.

You aren't expected to like everything you taste, and it's better to explore new wines and pour out a few, then to never taste anything new for fear of having to dump it out!

Tasting Fees

As mentioned earlier, wineries may offer a couple tasting menus with varying prices. It's a common practice for wineries to offer a tasting of special reserve wines, which typically cost more per bottle than the five or six wines that are on the standard tasting menu.

It is also common practice, for wineries to waive the tasting fee with a purchase of one or two bottles of wine. The tasting attendant will typically notify you of their policy during your wine tasting as a means to encourage you to buy their wine.

If you are on a budget or just don't feel comfortable with the idea of paying $40 for a tasting fee that won't be waived, I suggest looking online ahead of time and preparing your trip accordingly.

Tipping

When I worked as a tasting attendant, more often than not, I would receive cash and credit card tips from my customers.
I always felt appreciated and that I had provided exceptional service. And yet when I would go out wine tasting, I rarely saw anyone else leave cash tips.

Sure, they could have been tipping via credit card, but it made me curious as to what the proper tipping etiquette is after a wine tasting.

I learned that some wineries don't even allow their employees to receive tips, while others will have a tip jar on the counter. The rule of thumb is that you are not required or expected to leave a tip after tasting a flight of wines.

The exception of course being, if the tasting attendant went above and beyond to provide you with excellent customer service. For example, I would definitely tip someone who poured me additional wine that wasn't on the tasting list. Since tipping is not required nor expected, how much you decide to give is totally up to you. Personally, I use the same rules for restaurant tipping as I do for wine tasting.

Did you know? A tasting is about a one-ounce pour, so mathematically, after five or so tastings, you end up having one standard glass of wine!

Wine Tours

Are they worth the extra cost? If you want to add a little bit more adventure to your wine tasting, I highly suggest going on a wine tour. Most wineries offer tours of their facilities for an additional fee and it can be a really cool experience.

Some tours also take you through their vineyards and educate you on the soil, planting, and weather. Back in my *Moscato only* drinking days, I would go on wine tours for the touristy aspect of being at a winery. The more I learned about the winemaking process, the more I wanted to try different kinds of wine. I was curious how climate affected grapes from vintage to vintage.

I wanted to know what a white wine aged in stainless steel tasted like. And so on. If I had never gone on a wine tour, who knows where I'd be today. Perhaps still drinking Moscato from a 25-ounce Cabernet glass!

Wine Club Memberships

You can almost guarantee that you'll be pitched to join a wine club during your wine tasting. Don't ever feel pressured to make a decision on the spot, though. I've been pitched countless times, and my general practice is to take the pamphlet, let the tasting attendant finish their spiel, and say thank you. You don't even need to say, "I'll think about it," unless you are genuinely interested.

I never used to be interested in wine club memberships because I preferred buying wine from different wineries. I also assumed I would need to buy a wine fridge for all the wine that I'd need to store. My husband didn't like the idea of our power bill increasing for the sole purpose of keeping wine cool, so we ended up not buying a wine fridge.

It's a good thing we didn't because as time passed, I came to the realization that wine didn't last very long in my house. When I wanted to buy a few bottles of wine at a time, I'd just store the wine in my household fridge or in a relatively cool, dark place, like my bedroom closet.

During a visit to The Hess Collection in the Napa Valley, I fell in love with every single wine on the tasting list. I signed up for the three bottles per quarter membership, knowing that if we wanted to buy more wine, we'd get it at a discounted price.

Wineries usually offer several types of memberships, based off how many bottles of wine you want to commit to purchasing on a quarterly basis.

Being a member of a wine club gets you discounts on additional bottles of wine, complimentary tastings for you and your friends, and discounts on events hosted by the winery.

If you gravitate towards buying wine from a particular winery more often than any others, it might be worth doing the math, as I discovered that joining a wine club actually saved me money in the long run.

Wine Points and Awards

The title *award-winning* appeals to consumers and wineries alike because it establishes a sort of perceived value.

Statements next to price tags that read *Gold Medal SF Chronicle (2014)* or *97 points Wine Spectator* can increase wine sales and bring attention to the winery.

Journalistic publications like Wine Spectator and Wine Advocate have a panel of judges that award wines with points based on the wine's flavor, structure, and how well a wine reflects the grape varietal. Wines which have been entered into local and state competitions also have a panel of judges, but awards are given in the form of ribbons and medals.

Should you buy wine solely because it won an award or received high points? I'd say no. Not all wineries choose to enter their wine into competitions. You can definitely consider buying a wine that won a gold medal, but remember that wine is judged by a panel of people who might have completely different tastes in wine than you.

Sommelier

This is the title given to someone who has passed an exam on blind-tasting and a service practical, in addition to completing a written practical. You're most likely to find sommeliers working in the hospitality industry or in fine dining establishments.

This means the person who pours your wine during a tasting (whom I've been calling a *tasting attendant*) is most likely not going to be a certified sommelier. I've worked as a tasting attendant, and the level of wine expertise required was not remotely comparable to the level of knowledge that sommeliers have.

Bringing Your Own Bottle of Wine to a Restaurant

Sommeliers work at high-end restaurants, possibly coming to your table to recommend a bottle of wine to pair with your dinner. If you've ever glanced at a restaurant's wine list, you may have noticed two to three different prices listed next to each wine.

The lowest price is typically a half-glass (3 ounces), the middle price represents the cost of a full glass of wine (6 ounces), and the most expensive price is the cost of the bottle.

You'll also notice that some wines are only available by the bottle and some wines are only available by the glass.

I recommend choosing two to three wines you might be interested in drinking and asking the server if it's possible for you to taste them. Most servers have no problem allowing you to taste a couple of wines before deciding which one to order.

Another option is bringing your own bottle of wine to a restaurant and paying a fee for the restaurant to open it and serve it to you. Most high-end restaurants allow you to bring your own bottle of wine with a corkage fee (which sometimes costs more than the bottle of wine itself), so be sure to call ahead for the restaurant's corkage policies and fees.

CHAPTER 2

• • • • • •

HOW WINE IS MADE

Grapes have been grown and made into wine for thousands of years. Many religious ceremonies back in the day involved the drinking of wine due to its color resembling the blood of Jesus Christ. When idols were a big thing, Jewish rabbis were the only ones allowed to make wine, as a means of ensuring that the wine hadn't been made for the purpose of idolatry. In keeping with this tradition, anyone who observes Jewish dietary laws knows that only kosher food and beverages are consumed during Jewish religious ceremonies.

The process of making kosher wine is similar to the process of making non-kosher wine, with the exception of the winemaker having to be a Sabbath-keeping observer of the Jewish law. Most winemakers nowadays are not Sabbath-keeping rabbis and thus the wines they produce are considered non-kosher wines. However, it is still possible to find kosher wines at popular wine and beverage stores.

You'll also be able to find organic wine, boxed wine, and wine in aluminum cans. Heck, you can even find non-alcoholic wine (which more accurately should be called "dealcoholized wine" because it was once wine and then the alcohol was removed).

What do all these wines – kosher or not – have in common?

They all started as fruit on a vine.

Planting of the Vines

The winemaking process essentially begins with scouting out where to plant the grape vines. Ideally, grape vines are planted on sloping hillsides to gain the most exposure to sunlight and allow for proper rain drainage. Vines are strategically planted in rows, spaced about six-to-nine feet apart, depending on the quality of the soil.

As the vines grow, they are pruned during certain parts of the season as a means to control the direction of the vines, as well as to produce fresh new growth. It can take up to three years before grapevines yield any fruit. The amount of fruit (grapes) that a vine produces depends on how well the vines were taken care of, in addition to the weather conditions and if the grapevines are new or old.

New versus Old Vine

Grapevines are still considered new up to about 30 years of producing fruit. Past the 30-year mark, grapevines can be considered old, but it all depends on how much fruit the grapevines produce. As grapevines age, they yield less fruit, requiring more of the fruit to produce a 750 ml bottle of wine.

For example, if you were to drink an *Old Vine Zinfandel* from Lodi (a wine-growing region of California) and then drove an hour to the Shenandoah Valley to have a *New Vine Zinfandel*, you'd think you were drinking two different grape varietals.

Thus, it takes more grapes to produce a bottle of *old vine* wine than it does to produce a bottle of wine from grapevines that are only a decade or two old.

Harvest Time

Grapes are ready to be harvested when they've reached optimal levels of sugar, acidity, and tannins. Ultimately though, the wine-maker decides when the grapes should be harvested, as some grapes are intentionally left on the vine.

There are essentially two major ways to harvest grapes -- by machine or by hand -- and there are pros and cons to both methods.

Some wineries pride themselves on making wine from handpicked grapes, and there's good reason for it. First, when grapes are handpicked, only the ripe fruit is being harvested from the grapevines, which allows the unripe grapes to spend a little longer on the vine before being harvested.

Handpicking grapes off the vine is sometimes the only option for wineries, if machinery won't fit in between the vines or if the vineyards are located on really steep hills.

Some Old World wine regions don't even allow machine harvesting for the sake of keeping with tradition.

Machine harvesting comes in handy though, for wineries that have lots of grounds to cover and want to save on manual labor.

The unromantic thing about machine harvesting (besides the thought of a huge machine barreling down the rows of lush green vineyards) is that machine harvesting quite literally shakes the grapevines to harvest the grapes.

Not only does machine harvesting shake ripe grapes off the vines, but unripe grapes as well. And, you can guarantee other things will make into the grape bin including stems, leaves, insects, and hopefully no small animals.

Of course, all the non-grape roughage eventually gets filtered out, but the quality of the grapes can be affected by forceful shaking of the vine. The less intact the fruit, the more Sulphur is potentially used to preserve the grapes.

Which brings me to the topic of sulfites.

Sulfites

Sulphur dioxide (SO2) has anti-oxidative and anti-microbial properties that contribute to its ability to preserve wine grapes. Sulfites is the plural, all-inclusive term for compounds used in the winemaking process that contain the sulfite ion. All wines contain some level of sulfites, as these compounds naturally occur in wine grapes. Sulphur dioxide is also added to wine during different stages of the winemaking process.

Every bottle of wine with added sulfites produced in the U.S. has to include the statement *contains sulfites*. The statement *contains sulfites* is simply a warning for people who have sulfite sensitivities. It's the same type of warning used on the back of food packages that states, *made in a facility that processes wheat.* Both statements are a means to reduce an allergic reaction, not to freak you out.

Wine is actually relatively low in sulfites compared to other popular foods on the market. Dried fruit is super high in sulfites, as well as foods like molasses, grape juice, sauerkraut, and pickled vegetables.

If you break out in hives and need medical attention after consuming any of the foods mentioned above, you probably have a legitimate sulfite allergy.

Most of us, however, do not have a true allergy, and yet, we like to blame our headaches and flushed red cheeks on the sulfites that are in wine. Yes, flushed red cheeks after drinking wine with a high sulfite content may indicate a mild sensitivity. But that also means when you eat foods like molasses and dried fruit you will have the exact same reaction.

And, let's debunk the myth right now that red wine is the only kind of wine that contains sulfites, because as mentioned earlier, sulfites are a naturally-occurring compound in all grapes. That said, some wines do contain more sulfites than others. Sulfites are measured in ppm (parts per million), but the actual volume of sulfites is never disclosed on a bottle of wine. There are, however, ways you can go about buying wine that is potentially low in sulfites.

First, purchase wine that is estate-grown, produced, and bottled, which means the grapes didn't travel from one winery to the next. Hauling grapes in the backs of trucks can negatively impact the integrity of the grapes. As a means to reduce spoilage, wine grapes are sprayed with sulfites to protect them during travel.

Statements like *Estate-Grown, Produced, and Bottled* or *Vinted and Bottled by* can be found on the wine label. We will explain what statements like these mean in the bottling chapter, but just know that the less the grapes have to travel, the cleaner the wine, and the more likely it will contain the lowest level of sulfites.

Did you know? White wines have higher levels of sulfites compared to red wine, and sweet wines contain the most!

Primary Fermentation Process

Once wine grapes are harvested or brought into the winery from another source, they are ready to be turned into wine. You might have heard of an event called *The Crush*.

The Crush is the ever-so-anticipated time after grapes are harvested and sorted, where grapes are crushed and allowed to ferment in their skin and seeds. Natural yeasts immediately start to ferment the grapes the minute they are crushed. The winemaker can also add certain other yeasts to manipulate the flavor, aroma, and timing of the fermentation process.

All wines begin with stainless-steel fermentation for different periods of time. Red wine grapes used to make rosé wine macerate in their skins and seeds for only a few days. Red wine grapes used to make red wine ferment in their skins and seeds for up to two weeks.

Fermentation is basically done when most of the sugar has been turned into alcohol – which is an aspect of the winemaking process that the winemaker can control. White wine grapes naturally contain more sugar than red wine grapes, which means they will sit in stainless-steel containers for a longer period of time.

Secondary Fermentation Process

Nearly all wines go through a secondary fermentation process called malolactic fermentation (MLF). During MLF, lactic acid bacteria is added to wine to convert the naturally-occurring tart malic acid into creamy, drinkable wine.

Converting still wine to sparkling wine requires a secondary fermentation process that can happen one of two ways…. the *Champagne Method*, which involves the addition of yeast, sugar, and carbon dioxide to still wine that has been bottled, or the *Non-Champagne Method* (i.e. *Tank Method*) which involves the addition of yeast, sugar, and carbon dioxide to still wine that is in a large tank, having yet to be bottled.

Barrel Aging

Most red wines (and some white wines) are aged in oak barrels. Two of the most popular types of barrels used for aging wine are American and French oak. American oak softens the naturally harsh tannins in red wine and contributes to secondary flavors and aromas of toast and vanilla.

Full-bodied white wines like Chardonnay that are aged in American oak often taste like buttery popcorn, which is a distinguishing secondary flavor of most Chardonnays.

French oak contributes to a wines' silky texture and imparts secondary flavors of fruit into both red and white wines with floral undertones and baking spice.

Both red and white wines can age in French and American Oak, but for different lengths of time. Red wine, for example, can spend up to two years in an oak barrel while a white wine like Chardonnay, would spend much less time .

Did you know? Aging wine in porous oak barrels exposes the wine to oxygen, softening the overall structure of the wine.

Stainless-Steel Aging

The term *aging* in reference to wine is the action of letting a wine sit in a vessel for a particular period of time.

Before wine is bottled, it can either age in wooden barrels as mentioned earlier, or in stainless steel.

Stainless-steel aging retains the fruity characteristics of a wine and provides the wine with more floral flavors and aromas. Light-bodied, crisp white wines like Albarino and Pinot Grigio benefit from 100% stainless-steel aging. Other common styles of wines aged in stainless steel include Rosé and Champagne.

Light-bodied red and white wines which have been aged in stainless steel are often served chilled – making them popular summertime wines.

Each type of aging method has its pros and cons. Stainless steel is environmentally friendly (no tree cutting necessary) and costs less than oak barreling. However, if you tried to age a Cabernet Sauvignon wine in stainless steel, it would possibly be too bitter and harsh to drink. And oak aging of a fruity, sweet wine like Moscato would interfere with the wine's honeyed dessert qualities.

Clarification and Stabilization of Wine

Before wine is bottled, fining agents are added to wine to remove suspended particles and sediment that naturally occur during the fermentation/aging process.

Fining (clarifying) agents can also give the wine color, add to a wine's aroma, reduce bitterness, and contribute to the fermentation process.

Personally, I never knew fining agents existed until I did some research on whether or not wine was vegan. I quickly found out that the majority of wines on the market are not vegan. In fact, most of the clarifying agents used in wine are animal-based byproducts.

Casein (the main protein in mammal milk and cheese) and gelatin (collagen obtained from various animal parts) are common fining agents added to wine, as well as egg white and isinglass (a fish byproduct). This might not seem like a big deal to you, but as a vegan, I was pretty grossed out at the thought of those ingredients being in my wine. I found comfort in the fact, however, that fining /clarifying agents are filtered out of the wine before being bottled.

It's also important to note that if clarifying agents weren't added to wine, the wine would be cloudy and full of sediment. Not only do fining agents remove sediment, but they also remove things like dead yeast cells, bacteria, proteins, and various other compounds. If you are strictly vegan, or the idea of these clarifying agents being added to your wine (and filtered out) bothers you, there are wines available on the market labeled *unfiltered*. Wines labeled as *Organic* or *Biodynamic* are not necessarily vegan, so I'd suggest contacting the winery to learn about the production process and ingredients if you are concerned.

Bottling

Transporting wine from its aging vessels to the bottle is a complicated, delicate process. The proper equipment is necessary to keep the bottling process clean and streamlined.

Special care also needs to be made to reduce the wine's exposure to oxygen. When wine is exposed to too much oxygen before being bottled, its shelf life will be shortened.

With the proper machinery (and people who know what they are doing) the bottling process could look something like this:

When wine is ready to be bottled, empty wine bottles are loaded onto a conveyor belt to be washed. Nitrogen and argon are injected into each bottle to prevent oxidation while wine is being pumped through a filtration system. Auto levelers pump the precise amount of wine into each bottle. The wine then gets corked, capsuled, and labeled. Bottles are inspected for quality, and then packaged and are ready to go.

CHAPTER 3

• • • • • •

BOTTLING AND LABELING

Wine bottles were first designed in Burgundy, France back in the 19th century. The Burgundy-style bottle was made to hold the popular wines of that region, including oaked Chardonnay and Pinot Noir.

Bordeaux, France, a mere six-hour drive from Burgundy, is another popular wine-growing region, known for fuller-bodied Cabernet Sauvignon- and Merlot-based wines, and the dessert wine Sauternes. As a means to distinguish Bordeaux wines from neighboring wine regions, glassblowers designed cylindrical bottles with stout shoulders – accurately named the *Bordeaux-style* wine bottle.

Alsace-style wine bottles came into fruition in order to house light-bodied white wines like Riesling and Gewürztraminer from Alsace, France and Germany. *See my hand-drawn map below!*

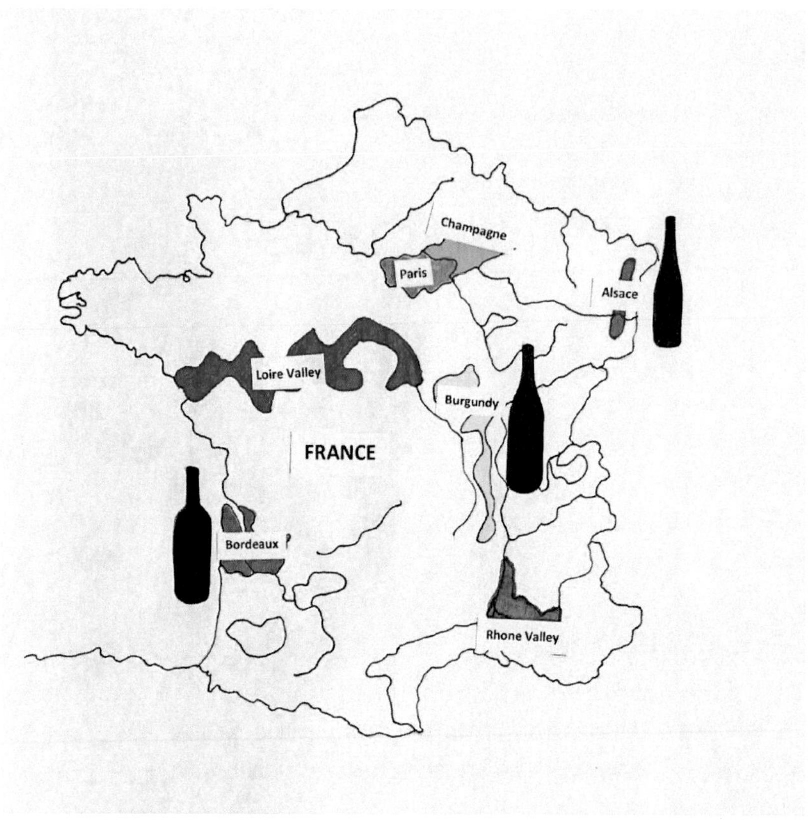

Jump to the 21st century and these three styles of wine bottles still house the same types of wine they were originally designed for!

You'll notice in the following picture that the Bordeaux bottle on the far left is a dark greenish-brown, the Burgundy bottle in the middle is yellowish-brown, while the Alsace-style bottle on the far right is bright green.

It is common to also see clear Alsace-style wine bottles housing light-bodied white wines that aren't as sensitive to light, but most wines age best in dark-colored glass where they can be protected from the damaging elements of light.

Despite the different colors and shapes of these three standard wine bottles, they all hold 750 ml of wine. One 750 ml wine bottle serves about five, 5-ounce glasses of wine.

Knowing how many glasses of wine a bottle holds is valuable information when determining how many bottles of wine you'll need to buy for events like weddings and dinner parties. Flip to *Chapter 8: How to Shop for Wine* for more information on how to buy wine for special occasions.

Another standard wine bottle size (which isn't pictured here) is a clear, 375 ml bottle reserved for dessert wines. One popular example of a dessert wine sold in a half bottle is Sauternes. The grapes used to make Sauternes are more concentrated with sugar and can be expensive to produce, which directly affects its retail value. The cost of a half bottle of Sauternes can be upwards of $50!

One more thing to mention about wine bottles is the punted bottom, found most commonly on Bordeaux and Burgundy-style wine bottles. Some Alsace-style wine bottles have punted bottoms, but they are often made flat-bottomed like the one shown in the picture. What's the purpose of punted bottoms on wine bottles? There are several theories, but not one definitive answer.

Historically, wine bottles were shaped with a punted bottom as a means to help the bottle stand upright. Current theories suggest that the punt helps disperse the sediment of the wine, as well as create a handhold for sommeliers trained in pouring wine.

Champagne bottles are designed with a punted bottom to withstand the immense pressure trapped inside the bottle during the secondary fermentation process--when carbon dioxide is added to the wine bottle.

Labeling

Have you ever walked down a wine aisle and picked out the bottle with the prettiest label? I certainly have. Perhaps it was my own ignorance for not educating myself on the verbiage of a wine label, but I'd literally just pick out the best-looking fifteen-dollar bottle of Moscato and hoped that it would taste good.

One of my goals for this book is to help you become a more educated wine consumer. It's important then, to understand what the most common words and phrases mean on a wine label.

Alcohol Percentage (ex: 14.5%)--Generally printed to the side of the label, the alcohol percentage (expressed as *ABV*, alcohol by volume) is the ratio of alcohol to all ingredients in one 5-ounce glass of wine.

Vintage--The year the grapes were picked.

Wine Region--The geographical area where the grapes were grown.

Producer--The winery who bottled the wine.

Varietal--The name of the grape.

Wine Name--Most often the name of the grape varietal like *Merlot*, but could also be a name given to the wine by the winemaker like *Wisdom of the Wise* when wine is made from a blend of grapes.

Government Warning--Required by United States Federal Law to be included on all alcoholic beverage containers. The government warning on the back of a wine bottle states:

1.) According to the Surgeon General, women should not drink alcoholic beverages during pregnancy because of the risk of birth defects.

2.) Consumption of alcoholic beverages impairs your ability to drive a car or operate machinery and may cause health problems.

UPC Code--The universal product code on the back of a bottle for tracking trade items in stores.

CONTAINS SULFITES--A U.S. government-regulated warning printed on all bottles of wine that contain added sulfites.

It can be confusing trying to find the name of a wine or determine where it came from, when wine labels vary across the board in color, style, formatting, and structure.

Here are two front-side photos of wine labels -- one from an Old World wine-growing region, and one from a New World wine-growing region, giving you an idea of where to find important information about the wine.

How to Read an Old World Wine Label

How to Read a New World Wine Label

On the back of each wine label, you will also see any ONE of the following statements underneath the government warning:

Produced and Bottled by--This means that at least 75% of the grapes in that bottle of wine were fermented at the facility of the winery that's selling the wine. The other percentage of grapes used to make the wine were most likely bought from other established wineries and blended at the facility.

Vinted and Cellared by--Most often, the grapes used to make the wine were purchased in bulk and blended with a very tiny percentage of the winery's own grapes. I've also learned that wines with this label can be highly manipulated. Things such as sugar and flavorings can be added, or other types of filtrations and pasteurization can happen at the winery that bought the wine.

Grown, Produced, and Bottled by--The grapes used to make wine with this label have to be grown on the winery's property or on properties (vineyards) that the winery owns or has control over. And, all wine-making processes took place on the winery's property.

Corked versus Screw-Off Tops

After bottles are filled with the perfect amount of wine, they are sealed, capsuled, and shipped off. Most wine bottles are sealed with a cork, but some are designed with an easy-to-remove screw-off top. Back in my early wine drinking days, I was under the impression that bottled wine with screw off tops were lower in quality compared to corked wine. It was only after I'd come home from wine tastings, with bottles of wine that had screw-off tops, that I realized the sealing method doesn't necessarily translate to the quality of the wine.

Sealing bottles with small pieces of cork is still the most popular way of bottling wine. Cork stoppers are made from the bark of a cork tree and have the ability to expand, creating a tight seal. However, there are several advantages screw-off tops have over cork stoppers.

First, wine that is bottled with cork seals can be affected by a chemical called trichloroanisole (TCA) that exists in the wood of the cork and can cause wine to go bad.

Second, wine bottles sealed with screw-off tops don't require a bottle opener. This is especially desirable when you are traveling and want to buy a bottle of wine to take back to the hotel.

Third, wine with screw-off tops might have the ability to actually age better. Corks can dry out, giving a small space (at the opening) for oxygen to enter.

CHAPTER 4

• • • • • •

FIVE COMPONENTS OF WINE

Turning grapes into the fermented beverage we call wine is a beautiful mixture of art, science, and tradition. As romantic as being a winemaker sounds, making great-tasting wine requires technique and a professional knowledge of viticulture.

All the ingredients that make up wine need to be closely monitored, regulated, and managed to create a well-balanced wine. Wine is actually made up of mostly water and other ingredients including ethanol, yeast, sugar, sulfur dioxide, clarifying agents, and tannins.

Collectively, these ingredients contribute to a wine's body, acidity, sugar level, alcohol level, and tannins.

The Body

If I were to pour you a glass of Champagne and asked you to describe it to me, what would you say? Perhaps you'd tell me that the Champagne tasted dry or sour.

Or if you were new to wine, maybe you'd compare Champagne to its non-alcoholic version--Martinelli's. And everything you would've just described to me would be correct.

There is technically no wrong way to describe a wine, because everyone's palate is different. Despite differences in taste, wine can structurally be categorized by its flavor profile, and the flavor profile of wine is determined by the volume of each of the five components described in this chapter.

Light-bodied white wines, for example, are named as such because they have low levels of alcohol and a higher sugar content compared to red wine. The low levels of alcohol and high levels of sugar contribute to how the wine feels in the mouth.

Sometimes alcohol is synonymous to a wine tasting hot, and that heat is a characteristic of a full-bodied red wine. Heat won't generally change the structure of a wine (unless it's left out in the direct sunlight for hours) but the texture of a red wine that's served at room temperature (65°-70°F) can feel different on the tongue than if it were served chilled at refrigerator temperature (31°-40°F).

Chilling wine can contribute to a wine's refreshing qualities, especially when served on a warm summer day. But as you'll read later on, red wine is typically best served at room temperature.

The body of wine also plays an important role in determining what kinds of foods to pair it with.

A high-alcohol red wine like Cabernet Sauvignon can taste hot and spicy, so pairing it with a creamy dish like lasagna would be superb.

A light-bodied white wine like Verdicchio has bright acidity and flavors of lemon and nuts which would complement a feta and walnut salad with lemon vinaigrette dressing.

A velvety smooth Merlot with soft tannins would enhance the flavor and textures of portabella mushroom steaks and golden mashed potatoes. Dessert wines like Moscato, Late Harvest Riesling, and Sauternes, are best paired with foods of similar sweetness like pie, tarts, fresh fruit, and biscotti.

Acidity

Remember that glass of Champagne you might have described as slightly sour? You were more accurately describing the acidity level of the wine. And interestingly enough, there are three major kinds of acid that exist in wine: tartaric acid, malic acid, and citric acid.

Malic acid is primarily involved in malolactic fermentation, which as you recall, is the process of adding lactic acid to the wine to convert the tart, naturally-occurring malic acid into a softer, smoother wine.

Tartaric acid is a naturally-occurring acid found in grape skins. Tartaric acid contributes not only to the acidity of wine, but it also plays a major role in the chemical stability of wine.

Citric acid is the most familiar, as it's the sour ingredient that exists in all citrus fruits.

If you've ever bitten into the flesh of a lemon, you've tasted citric acid at its finest. Being that this acid is super intense, it's carefully used in the winemaking process and is only added after the primary fermentation process. If citric acid was added to the wine during the primary fermentation process, it would react harshly with the yeast and produce an unwanted product called acetic acid (i.e. vinegar). Thus, all three of these acids play an important role in creating a well-balanced wine.

Did you know? Cream of tartar-- an ingredient used in baking--is the salt form of tartaric acid.

Tannins

Tannins are naturally-occurring, organic polyphenols that work like antioxidants in the body, fighting off free radicals. Free radicals are molecules formed through normal human metabolism as well as a byproduct of unhealthy foods.

Tannins exist in grape skins, oak barrels, and foods like walnuts, cranberries, chocolate, herbs, and spices. All these foods have high antioxidant values, because the higher the tannin content in a food or beverage, the better the source of antioxidants.

The longer grapes macerate in their skins and ferment in a wine barrel, the higher the level of tannins in the wine. This is why red wines are considered healthier than white wines when speaking specifically to the volume of antioxidants.

Tannins exist in the grape skins of all wine grapes. Red wine grapes, however, macerate in their skins and seeds for a much longer period of time than white wine grapes, thus increasing the health value of red wine. Red wine is also more likely to be aged oak barrels.

Tannins also are responsible for the dry feeling you get in your mouth after drinking red wine. Tannins tend to have an astringent characteristic that is often described as *bitter*, which gives red wine the keen ability to pair well with foods like radicchio, walnuts, heavily-spiced vegetables, and pasta dishes.

Did you know? Tannins in red wine literally remove proteins from the tongue, which contributes to its dry mouth feeling.

Sugar Level

Sugar exists in ALL wines. The level of naturally-occurring sugar in wine is highly determined by the grape itself. Red wine grapes tend to be lower in sugar and produce wines higher in alcohol. White wine grapes tend to be higher in sugar, producing lower alcohol wines.

Winemakers have the ability to manage the sugar content in wine by controlling how much and what kind of yeasts are added to the wine.

We will discuss wine's sugar content in a little more depth, in chapter 10, but just know that if you are a wine drinker who is trying to reduce your overall sugar intake, a full-bodied red wine would be your best bet!

Alcohol

What would wine be without alcohol??? Umm… non-alcoholic? Indeed, it is possible to have wine that has been dealcoholized, meaning that it once contained alcohol.

But you might find it interesting to know that once wine grapes are crushed, they start to produce ethanol from the naturally-occurring yeast that exists in the grape skins.

As discussed earlier, additional yeasts are added to wine to turn grape sugar into alcohol, and this process is controlled by the winemaker. In chapter 10, we will discuss how alcohol affects the over health of wine.

CHAPTER 5

• • • • • •

FLAVOR PROFILES OF WINE

Wine is often referred to as red or white, but wines run the gamut in color. White wines can be gold, greenish-yellow, or so transparent that they look like water. And wines labeled red can actually look purple or maroon. Some red wines almost look inky black in certain lighting. Pink wine, which is in a class of its own, is made from red wine grapes, and ranges in color from strawberry-red to dark pink and salmon colored hues.

Despite the varying color schemes of wine, it is indeed still possible to group certain wines together based on similar flavor profiles. You may have heard statements like, "Red wine pairs best with steak," and, "White wine pairs really well with fish." And if you're vegetarian, you'd have no idea if these statements were actually true, nor would you know *why* those foods paired best with the suggested wine.

In this chapter we will discuss **nine** different categories of wine, the common characteristics of each, and which foods pair best -- taking into consideration the wine's tannins, alcohol level, sugar level, acidity, and body.

Let's begin with sparkling wine.

Sparkling Wine

Served in a tall, skinny wine glass with tiny bubbles that tickle your nose, sparkling wine exemplifies sheer beauty and elegance. The very fact that sparkling wine is carbonated, sets it apart from any other style of wine.

Beginning as still wine, sparkling wine is created by adding carbon dioxide during the secondary fermentation process. The most traditional secondary fermentation process is called *The Champagne Method*.

The Champagne Method involves the addition of carbon dioxide to produce carbonation in still wine that's been bottled. *The Tank Method is* another secondary fermentation process, where carbon dioxide is added to still wine in tanks to produce carbonation *before* it's bottled.

For sparkling wine to be labeled as a true Champagne, the winemaking process has to follow some specific guidelines.

First, grapes used to make Champagne must be grown in the Champagne region of France. Second, Champagne is only made from three specific grapes: Pinot Noir, Pinot Meunier, and White Chardonnay. When Champagne is made with red wine grapes only, it's titled Blanc De Noir (French for *white from black).* Champagne made solely from the White Chardonnay grape is called Blanc De Blanc *(*French for *white from white).*

When describing Champagne, as with any wine, it's important to understand *how* to express what you taste in the wine. For example, if someone was to ask me what a Champagne tastes like, I'd say that it possesses flavors of apples, nuts, and freshly-baked bread.

Wine can be described by its **aroma**, as well. Common primary aromas of Champagne include Jasmine flowers, lemon, and pear. And guess what? There are secondary aromas that exist in wine as well.

The wine industry classifies these secondary aromas as a wine's **bouquet.** The term *bouquet* more accurately describes the characteristics of wine attributed by the fermentation and aging processes. So, we could say that Champagne is known for its nutty, yeasty bouquet.

Sparkling wine is unique in the sense that it doesn't require a corkscrew to open. Without any special devices, it might seem simple enough to open up a bottle of bubbly, but there is a technique to opening a bottle of wine in which the contents are under pressure.

Tips to opening a bottle of Champagne:

- Chill the wine before serving
- Remove the wire cage
- Hold the bottle at a 45-degree angle
- Using a thin dishtowel or washcloth, slowly twist the cork, keeping the bottle study as you prepare for a large popping sound
- While holding the flute glass at an angle, slowly pour the wine into the glass until it is three-quarters full
- Smell, sip, toast... ENJOY!!

I highly recommend investing in a Champagne bottle stopper. You'll quickly find out that a Champagne cork expands upon opening, so you can't reseal the bottle with the same cork. I use to try and get away with using regular wine stoppers to seal leftover sparkling wine, but discovered that the carbonation pushes wine stoppers out the top of the bottle. Champagne bottle stoppers are designed with clamps to prevent this problem, thus creating a tighter seal.

Did you know? Most of the sparkling wines in the U.S. are considered Brut. Brut is a style of Champagne that has tiny bubbles, a flavor profile that is slightly sweet, and low residual sugar.

Common characteristics of sparkling wine: bubbles, contents under pressure, sugar levels ranging from super dry to sweet
Examples of wines in this category: Champagne, Prosecco, Lambrusco, Cava, Cremant, Sekt
Wine glass: flute glass
Pairing partners: nuts, cheese, crackers, creamy dips and sauces, pretty much anything and everything

Full-bodied White Wine

Full-bodied white wines have the highest level of alcohol (13.5%-14.5% ABV) compared to other white wines. They taste rich and creamy and are often heavily-oaked. Chardonnay is the perfect example of wine in this category, as it exemplifies flavors of oak and butter which contribute to its richness.

As discussed earlier, malolactic fermentation is the process by which a wine's naturally-occurring tart malic acid is replaced with lactic acid, which contributes to the creamy mouthfeel you get when drinking full-bodied white wines.

Saying that a wine is *heavily-oaked* simply means that it tastes like it was sitting in the trunk of an oak tree for a while. This might sound intense, but aging wine in oak imparts secondary flavors and aromas which contribute to the overall structure and body of the wine.

Full-bodied white wines pair well with foods whose cooking methods intensify their flavors, such as roasting, braising, stewing, and grilling.

Common flavors and aromas of full-bodied white wine: toasted oak, citrus, apple, pear, buttery popcorn
Examples wines in this category: Viognier, Chardonnay, Vouvray, Marsanne
Wine glass: white wine glass (stemmed or stemless)
Pairing partners: grilled portabella mushrooms, creamy sauces and dressings, corn chowder, Gruyere cheese, hazelnuts, couscous with dried apricots

Medium-bodied White Wine

Medium-to-light-bodied white wines spend most of their time aging in stainless steel at low temperatures of around 59°F. White wines in this category are often described as crisp due to their slightly lower alcohol content, time spent in stainless steel, and preservation of naturally-occurring malic acid.

Wine produced from different wine-growing regions will taste different, despite being made from the same grape varietal.

Old World Sauvignon Blanc for example, can possess flavors of lime, minerals, and asparagus (I know, kinda weird), while Sauvignon Blanc from New World wine-growing regions like the U.S. and New Zealand, can exemplify flavors and aromas of tropical fruit, honeysuckle, and grass. Knowing common characteristics of wines from specific regions can help you determine which wines will pair best with your food.

Common flavors and aromas of medium-bodied white wine: citrus, herbs, pineapple, stone fruits, flint, with hints of grass
Example wines in this category: Pinot Gris, unoaked Sauvignon Blanc, Gruner Veltliner, Verdicchio, Soave, Vino Verdhe, Albarino, Chablis, Trebbiano, White Rioja
Wine glass: white wine glass (stemmed or stemless)
Pairing partners: bitter greens salad, marmalade, vinaigrette dressings, grilled foods, Thai, Indian, Moroccan, roasted vegetables, goat's and sheep's milk cheeses

Did you know? Trebbiano wine grapes are used to make white balsamic vinegar!

Light-bodied White Wine

Delicate white wines with a low alcohol percentage and predominant floral aromas are most often described as light-bodied white wines. Many of the wines in this category are known for being great *beginner wines* due to their residual sugar levels being just slightly lower than dessert wines.

Light-bodied white wines are aged in stainless steel to retain the natural fruit flavors, and undergo malolactic fermentation contributing to the wine's soft and creamy texture.

Some light-bodied white wines have a slight effervescence which is a distinguishing characteristic of medium-to-light bodied white wines. Being lower in alcohol, soft white wines (another term for light-bodied) are often served chilled and make the perfect accompaniment to lighter-fare foods like bruschetta, salads with vinaigrette dressing, any of the appetizers featured in this book, and salmon.

One of the most notable features of light-bodied white wines is their ability to pair with highly acidic foods and spicy ingredients such as lime, jalapeno, black pepper, and hot sauce.... Tacos anyone?

Common flavors and aromas of light-bodied white wine: white peach, apricot, tropical fruit, Jasmine flowers, spice
Example wines in this category: dry or semi-sweet Riesling, Gewürztraminer, Torrontes, Muscadet, dry or sweet Pinot Blanc, Chenin Blanc
Wine glass: white wine glass, Riesling glass, glass tumbler
Pairing partners: vinaigrette dressing, spicy curry, stir fry, sauerkraut, tacos, salty foods like potato chips (*try it!),* Gruyere and Cheddar cheeses

Rosé [Pink] Wine

Oh, Pink wine!! How beautiful you are sitting in a stemless glass!
You are so often misunderstood.
Your personality can be sweet with a playful effervescence.

You can be calm and still, with a dryness that invites the
creamiest of cheeses.
Love and hate relationship with you, Rosé.

The colors of rosé wines are as vast as a rose garden; ranging in color from light and dark pinks to resembling light-bodied red wines and sometimes even looking gray.

Rosé wines are made from red wine grapes, but don't taste like red wines for several important reasons…

- Minimal contact with red wine grape skins during fermentation, contributes to a light, rose-colored wine.
- Rosé wines are fermented in stainless steel (versus oak) contributing to a very low level of tannins.
- Rosé wine is generally considered to have a medium-to-low alcohol content, ranging from 11% to 13.5% ABV.
- Rosé wine can be sweet **or** dry.
- Rosé wine is best served chilled.

Some rosé wines are blends, and others are single varietal wines-- both contribute to a wide variety of flavors, ranging from herbaceous to super fruity.

Rosé wines are generally paired with lighter-fare foods and are definitely a must during the summertime!

Common flavors and aromas of rosé wine: strawberry, watermelon, cherry, dried cranberries, melon, some have herbal notes with lemon, lime, and a mineral backbone
Example wines in this category: Pinot Noir Rosé, Vin Gris, Syrah Rosé, Rosé of Cabernet Sauvignon
Wine glass: Rosé glass**,** Riesling glass, white wine glass, red wine glass, glass tumbler

Pairing partners: grilled vegetables, pear and cranberry salad, BBQ, cream cheese, feta, Greek food

Did you know? Rosé and white wines don't require ample time to breathe, thus it typically isn't necessary to let the wine decant for hours or swirl the wine around in your glass.

Full-bodied Red Wine

Full-bodied red wine is the ultimate dinner wine. Coming in at an upwards of 14% ABV, full-bodied red wines are high in tannins and low in residual sugar, with moderate acidity. If you've ever sipped a red wine and thought it tasted bitter, you were tasting the flavor of tannins in the wine. It's the high level of tannins in red wine that dry out the mouth, causing you to salivate for the next bite of food--thus creating a food and wine relationship that enhances the dining experience.

Full-bodied red wines benefit from being exposed to oxygen shortly before being consumed. Pouring wine into a decanter and letting it sit for 30 minutes or so gives the wine enough time to be brought to room temperature.

Allowing wine to come to room temperature exposes the wine's aromatic molecules to oxygen. Swirling wine around in the glass releases the aromatic molecules into the air and enhances the taste of the wine.

Full-bodied red wines also have an incredible ability to age. Aging wine means allowing it to sit unopened in a cool, dark place for any given period of time.

Aging full-bodied red wines for several years can soften the harsh tannins, resulting in a more velvety, smooth-textured wine.

Common flavors and aromas of full-bodied red wine: dark red fruit, spice, bell pepper, herbs, hints of coffee, vanilla, roses, tobacco
Example wines in this category: Syrah, Shiraz, Petite Syrah, Cabernet Sauvignon, Merlot, Malbec, Petite Verdot, Tannat, Mourvedre, Nebbiolo, Barolo, Barbaresco, Rioja
Wine Glass: Bordeaux glass, Cabernet Sauvignon glass, glass tumbler
Pairing Partners: truffle oil, bitter foods like radicchio, blue cheese, mint, kale, bell pepper, black pepper, arugula, stewed meats and vegetables, braised root vegetables, roasted tomato sauces

Did you know? Cabernet Sauvignon is one of the most demanded wines on the market, thus also making it one of the most expensive.

Medium-bodied Red Wine

[I am using the term *medium-bodied* for simplicity's sake, as a collective term to describe the characteristics of wine that are between full-bodied and light-bodied.]

Perhaps, some would argue that medium-bodied red wines are the best dinner-pairing wines, due to their moderate acidity, medium-to-low alcohol content (13.5%), and relatively low tannins.

Medium-bodied red wines spend very little time aging in oak barrels to preserve their natural fruit flavors and are known for their ability to improve with age.

Interestingly, a few of the most popular medium-bodied red wines are known by more than one name. New World wines made from 100% Sangiovese grapes are sold and marketed as Sangiovese. Old World wines made from 100% Sangiovese grapes are sold and marketed by the wine-growing region.

Throughout this book I've been highlighting both New and Old World wines as a means to bring attention to the vast differences in a wine's flavor and structure, despite being made from essentially the same grape.

For example, a California Sangiovese wine from the Sierra Foothills will taste fruity, with moderate acidity, and low tannins. While a Brunello di Montalcino wine (made with 100% Sangiovese grapes) from Italy, will have bold fruit flavors, high tannins, and high acidity.

Common flavors and aromas of medium-bodied red wine: black currants, bing cherries, blackberries, plum, mocha, pomegranate, minerals, herbs, baking spice
Example wines in this category: Barbera, Cabernet Franc, Valpolicella, Grenache, Zinfandel, Sangiovese, Carignan, Chianti, Tempranillo, Dolcetto, Mencia, Brunello di Montalcino
Wine glass: Bordeaux glass, glass tumbler
Pairing partners: pizza, burgers, grilled vegetables, ketchup, balsamic vinegar, lentils, risotto, mushrooms, black beans, Parmesan and Asiago cheeses

Did you know? Oak-barrel aging bumps up the price of wine.

Light-bodied Red Wine

Light-bodied red wines are naturally juicy, low in tannins, and excellent served slightly chilled.
These are what I like to call your *midday wines*. Being low in alcohol (10%-13% ABV) light-bodied red wines pair really well with lunch-style foods like sandwiches, salads, cheese, and crackers.

In my opinion, light-bodied red wines are excellent transition wines. If you currently prefer Moscato over a full-bodied red, I recommend trying any of the wines in this category.

Lighter-bodied red wines are often aged in stainless steel or spend very little time aging in oak barrels to preserve their natural fruit flavors.

Common flavors and aromas of light-bodied red wine: candied cherry, raspberry, cranberry, raisin, banana, strawberry, with some herbal and earthy notes
Example wines in this category: Gamay, Pinot Noir, Frappato, Beaujolais, Zweiglet
Wine glass: Burgundy glass, Pinot Noir glass, glass tumbler
Pairing partners: pasta with fresh herbs, tomato bruschetta, Gouda and Parmigiano Reggiano cheeses, pizza, grilled foods

Dessert Wine

Dessert wine contains the highest level of residual sugar compared to any other category of wine. You might assume that since dessert wines are high in sugar they will be correspondingly low in alcohol.

The alcohol content of dessert wines can vary, however, ranging from 5% to 13.5% ABV-- with some fortified wines being as high as 20% ABV.

The alcohol percentage in wine legally has to be included on each wine label, but the amount of other ingredients in wine doesn't have to be disclosed. Sugar in wine is measured in *brix* – a food industry measurement that doesn't compare to standard measuring units typically included on an ingredient label. If you want to know *how much* sugar is in a particular glass of wine, you'll have to contact the producer of the wine directly.

There are, however, ways you can determine the sugar level in wine without knowing the exact numbers. Sweet wines like Late Harvest Riesling, Sauternes, Ice Wine, and Port are generally sold in half-sized bottles, and cost more than a 750 ml bottle of mainstream Moscato. The size of the serving glass meant for a particular dessert wine is another clue as to how sweet the wine will be.

Moscato for example, can be served in a standard white wine glass, while a more concentrated wine like Sauternes will be served in a 2-3-ounce sipping glass.

Late harvest Riesling and Sauternes are two examples of sweet wines made from grapes affected by a fungus formally known as *botrytis cinerea* and informally known as *Noble Rot*.

Noble Rot isn't a pretty sight. Type those words into a Google search engine and the images may disturb you.

Noble rot is a fungus that grows on grapes, essentially causing the fruit to go rotten. Have you ever seen moldy strawberries? Yeah, it's like intentionally wanting that to happen.

Noble Rot requires certain conditions (like humidity) to properly penetrate the skins of wine grapes. Grapes affected by Noble Rot become dehydrated and are individually-picked to be made into a sweet, viscous, honey dominant wine. It requires a large number of grapes affected by Noble Rot to produce one half-sized bottle of wine.

Late Harvest is a simple term meaning that grapes were left on the vine past harvest, to be affected by botrytis cinerea (Noble Rot). Not all grape varietals have the ability to be affected by this fungus, as the fungus requires relatively thin-skinned grapes to penetrate through. Riesling grapes are one of the most popular grapes used to make late harvest wine because of their thin skins and naturally high acidity – which balances out the high concentration of sugar.

Sauternes is a late harvest wine made from Semillon grapes grown in the Sauternes region of South Bordeaux, France. Late harvest wine made from Semillon grapes grown in New World wine regions like Washington are labeled *Late Harvest Semillons*.

Ice wine is made from grapes that were left on the vine to freeze. Not all grapes can be made into ice wine, as the grapes themselves need to be able to sustain the cooler climates.

The tricky thing about making ice wine is that the weather conditions have to be nearly perfect, allowing the grapes to freeze before being affected by Noble Rot. Once the grapes are frozen, they are then harvested in sub-zero temperatures and pressed immediately. The small amount of juice produced by the frozen grapes is super-concentrated and very sweet.

Ice wine is sold in half-sized bottles at a relatively high cost. The most expensive ice wines come from Canada and Germany, while ice wines produced in the U.S. tend to be more affordable.

I personally had the experience of sampling a very expensive ice wine from Germany at a friend's house. Being that I had no education on the proper way of drinking this particular wine, I remember pouring it into a regular-sized wine glass, taking a sip, hating it, and then pouring it down the drain.

Needless to say, the person who bought the bottle of wine wasn't very happy watching me pour this expensive novelty wine down the drain. Whoops. I learned that when it comes to drinking expensive wines, even if you don't like it, drink it. Or, find someone else to drink it for you. Just don't throw it out!

Despite already being high in sugar, sweet wines are actually designed to be paired with sweet foods. Matching similar flavors and textures of sweet wine with desserts can make for an extraordinary after-dinner experience. In the recipe section of this book, I pair a light, sweet white wine like Moscato with an apple crostada dessert because the flavors, textures, and aromas complement one another.

Thick, sweet wines like Late Harvest Riesling, Sauternes, and Ice Wine make for striking companions to soft cheeses as an aperitif or after-dinner dessert. They are also delicious when drizzled on top of fresh fruit, ice cream, and pound cake.

Fortified wines are a different style of dessert wine, as they contain spirits like brandy, which increases their alcohol content by a fair margin (18% + ABV). Port, Madeira, Sherry, Marsala, and Vermouth are popular fortified wines served with cheese as an aperitif or with chocolate as an after-dinner dessert.

Common flavors and aromas of dessert wine: green apple, pear, peach, hazelnut, apricot, honey, elderflowers

Example wines in this category: Moscato, Late Harvest Riesling, Sauternes, Vin Santo, Ice Wine, Port, Madeira, Sherry, Marsala, Vermouth
Wine glass: Port glass, Sherry glass, sipping glass, white wine glass
Pairing partners: apple pie, apricot strudel, soft cheeses, fresh fruit, vanilla bean ice cream, pound cake, chocolate cake with warm raspberry sauce

CHAPTER 6

• • • • • •

OLD AND NEW WORLD WINE

Europe and the Middle East are considered the birthplaces of wine. Dating back to biblical times, these two countries, along with other wine-growing regions of the world like Portugal, Greece, and Spain, have been making wine for thousands of years.

The wine industry classifies wine from these regions as *Old World*. Wine-growing regions like the United States, Argentina, Australia, and Chile are considered *New World* wine countries because they haven't been making wine for as long.

Old and New World wine countries will inevitably produce different-tasting wines. New World wine countries tend to have hotter climates, which produces fuller-bodied fruity wines, with higher alcohol content. Old World wine countries tend to have cooler climates, producing lighter-bodied wines with more of a vegetal character and low alcohol content.

Old World wine countries also have very strict wine-making rules, sticking to more traditional ways of producing wine.

Meanwhile, New World wine countries have freedom to experiment with their winemaking processes. This freedom in production carries over to the wine label, as New World wine labels run the gamut in color, description, and order of information.

Old World wine labels, though harder to read, can actually provide more detail about the respective wine-growing region compared to New World wine labels. Old World wine labels also tend to include a governmentally-regulated stamp of quality.

In the recipe section of this book, I list both New and Old World wine-pairing options to encourage you to taste a variety of wines from different wine-growing regions.

Here's a quick reference chart to show you the differences between New and Old World wine.

New World Wine	**Old World Wine**
Countries: United States, Australia, Chile, Argentina, South America, New Zealand, South Africa	**Countries**: France, Germany, Italy, Spain, Austria, Hungary, Middle East, Portugal
Freedom to experiment	Traditional
Associate their wines by grape varietal and producer	Distinguish their wines by region in which the grapes were grown
Upfront flavors of fruit	Subtle and Complex

CHAPTER 7

• • • • • •

WINE GLASSES

It may come as no surprise to you that wine glasses differ in shape and size. I remember restocking the wine glass shelf at Crate and Barrel, when I worked there as a seasonal employee, and being absolutely mesmerized at the vast array of crystal glassware.

Years later, I learned that wine glasses are actually designed to accentuate the flavors of particular kinds of wine. Take a 25-ounce Cabernet glass for example. It's designed with a huge bowl on top of a slender stem, to give full-bodied red wines the most exposure to oxygen.

The standard drink size of wine doesn't change, however, with the size of the wine glass. But, have you ever just poured 5 ounces of wine into a 25-ounce glass? It looks like nothing. I guarantee you'll be consuming more than just one standard serving of wine, if you are drinking your wine from a balloon-style wine glass.

Not to mention the fact (except I guess I AM mentioning it) that full-bodied red wines are well beyond 12% ABV… another knock against what the *Dietary Guidelines for Americans* label as one standard drink.

I even find myself telling people that I typically only have *one glass of wine* a night. Which doesn't sound like much, in theory, but what size is that wine glass??

I simply want to make you aware that *one glass of wine* isn't the same thing as *one standard drink*. We will discuss why this matters in chapter 10, when we talk about the sugar and alcohol content in wine.

You Bought It, so Don't Break It

I don't know about you, but I've broken a lot of glassware in my lifetime. And as much as I know that glass is technically replaceable, it's still upsetting (not to mention potentially dangerous) when it breaks.

Accidents can happen, but there are plenty of things to do to prevent glassware from breaking as easily. The first step is actually to USE your glassware. If you think that not using your nice stemware is preserving it, why even own it?! An earthquake could come along, and shake your shelves, breaking all your stemware, and it would be pretty disheartening if you hadn't ever used the glassware that broke, right?!

Indeed, if it's taking up space in your place, you should definitely use it!

Second, inspect your glassware before pouring wine into it. Glasses can be cracked without fully breaking, in which case, safely dispose of the fractured glassware to prevent it from being used.

Third, place stemware on a flat surface and hold the stem of the glass while pouring in the wine. If you plan to take your glass of wine into the living room, create a safe place for it to be set down where it won't be bumped over by animals and children.

One suggestion is to buy a set of glass tumblers for everyday use and save the goblet-style glassware for dinner at the table.

When it's time to wash empty wine glasses, DO NOT set the glasses in the sink! I always set my wine glasses off to the side of the sink in a place where they won't be bumped over. And, always hand wash your wine glasses.

Resist the urge to put them in the dishwasher with everything else, as they could clank around and break. When handwashing your wine glasses, gently sponge the inside (if you can) and outside of the glass without forcing your hand into the glass to wash it. Once cleaned, place the stemware on a drying rack, and if possible, towel-dry to prevent water-droplet residue.

Now, with those tips on how to care for your glassware, let's explore some popular styles of wine glasses that were mentioned in the flavor profile chapter!

Flute Glass: Reserved specifically for Champagne and sparkling wine, the tall, narrow shape of flute glassware preserves the wine's bubbles by retaining the carbon dioxide in the wine.

White Wine Glass: The *U-shaped* bowl of this particular glassware directs the aromas of white wine to the mouth and nose, while retaining a cooler temperature and less exposure to oxygen.

Cabernet Glass: Goblet-style wine glass with a large bowl and a wide-open rim. Any full-bodied red wine can be served in this glass.

Bordeaux Glass: Originally designed to accentuate the flavors of Bordeaux-style red wines from Southwestern, France, this narrow-rimmed glass with a long cylindrical body, can be used for a variety of red and white wines.

Burgundy Glass: Goblet-style wine glass with a narrow top and a medium to large bowl, shaped for aromatic, juicy wines like Pinot Noir.

Riesling / Rosé Glass: Round-bottomed bowl with a tapering side and a curve-lipped rim designed to guide sweet, aromatic wines to the tip of the tongue.

French Wine Glass: Wide-open rim and a tapering body. Both red and white wines can be served in this glass.

Port Glass: Narrow-rimmed wine glass with a 10-ounce *U-shaped* bowl designed for dessert wines.

Dessert Wine Glass: the 2-3-ounce wine glass shown here, is designed for aromatic and complex dessert wines like Sauternes, Ice Wine, and Late Harvest Riesling. Fortified wines can be poured into this glass as well, but many have their own special glass.

Please Note: This most certainly not an exclusive list of wine glassware. These glasses will, however, meet the needs of most everyday wine drinkers!

CHAPTER 8

• • • • • •

HOW TO SHOP FOR WINE

I was at a neighborhood grocery store browsing around their small wine department, when my eyes fell upon a Cabernet Sauvignon from Chile. It was on the bottom shelf and priced at $3.99. I remember thinking, *"Damn that's cheap!"* and was immediately curious if the wine was *actually* any good.

Price is often associated with the quality of wine, so I wasn't really expecting much from a bottle that cost less than five bucks. I was pleasantly surprised, however, to be met with a delicious red wine that I'd definitely buy again.

So, what defines a quality wine?

To me, a well-balanced wine is the first indicator of quality. A balanced wine is where all five components of a wine (acidity, sugar, alcohol, tannins, and body) blend together so well that not one component of the wine stands out. I also equate quality to wine that is estate-grown, produced, and bottled.

As mentioned earlier, when grapes are grown on the same property as the winemaking process, the level of added sulfites (for preservation) is greatly reduced.

How do you know if your wine was made on the property of the winery selling it? The information on the back of the wine bottle will tell you! Here is where we explain the meaning of common statements found on the back of the wine label.

You will see any of the following titles in bold:

***Imported by*:** The name of the winery or distributer who shipped the wine to the U.S. Included on every Old World bottle of wine.

***Cellared and Bottled by**:* The wine was purchased from a producer (not disclosed on the wine label) and aged and bottled on the estate.

***Produced and Bottled by*:** By law, 75% of the wine in the bottle has to be crushed, fermented, and bottled on the estate.

***Vinted and Bottled by*:** The wine was purchased in bulk and bottled at the winery.

***Made and Bottled by*:** Only 10% of the wine in the bottle was crushed, fermented, and bottled on the estate.

***Estate Grown, Produced, and Bottled*:** The best of the best. All stages of the winemaking process were done on the estate.

You are most often going to see *Vinted or Made by* on labels of wine that were produced by large corporations.

There are several major wine-producing companies that own popular wine labels such Robert Mondavi and Louis Martini--both of whom have wineries located in the Napa Valley.

For the sake of business and consistency, companies will produce the same-tasting wine year after year--which if you think about it, isn't the reality of wine.

Handcrafted wine tastes like the true vintage of the grape. When wine is produced in small batches, more attention is paid to every aspect of the winemaking process, including allowing the wine to taste just a little bit different year after year.

Cost of Wine

Wine that's produced in large quantities tends to cost less because it costs less to produce, but the quality of the wine isn't the same. Personally, I'm all about supporting independent wineries as much as I can. The money you spend on a handcrafted bottle of wine is supporting the farmers, the winemaker, the barrel maker, the cork, the label, the travel cost, and everything else in between.

When you're shopping for a bottle of wine, it's important to know that wine is categorized on the shelf by price range. Much like how cold cereal is presented to the consumer, the most expensive product is on the top shelf. The middle two or three shelves are reserved for mid-priced wine, leaving the bottom shelf for the cheapest wines.

While strolling down the wine aisle, you might notice wines that are packaged in boxes and aluminum cans. Boxed wine has a bad reputation for being a cheap way to get drunk.

Interestingly, I did the math to see how much cheaper boxed wine was compared to a low-to-mid range quality wine, and actually it wasn't that much cheaper!

Wine in aluminum cans is somewhat of a novelty thing, but I personally don't recommend it. I find that wine in aluminum cans have an unpleasant tinny/metal aftertaste.

Wines by Occasion

Let's say you are responsible for buying wine for a special occasion. If you've never seen the likes of a wine department, or only purchased wine for yourself, have no fear. I've included a list of popular holidays and suggested wines for each occasion.

Here are my recommendations:

New Year's: Champagne, baby! Wine under pressure is a MUST for this occasion. The stream of tiny bubbles in a classy flute glass creates an ambiance to which no other wine can attest to. You can choose the color of the sparkling wine, as well. If you want pink, I suggest a Mumm Blanc de Noir or any other mid-priced sparkling wine. Special occasions call for special wine, so no bottom-shelf shopping here.

Easter: Light-bodied white and rosé wines are prefect for late afternoon Easter dinners. They are low in alcohol and pair nicely with a wide variety of different foods. I'd suggest a dry Riesling, a crisp Sauvignon Blanc, or an Old World Rosé.

Valentine's Day: Deep, rich ruby reds and pinks that range in color from salmon to dark pink give rise to top-shelf red and rosé wines.

This is the holiday to buy that handcrafted bottle of Cabernet Sauvignon or pick up a few extra bottles of Rosé at your local winery.

Mother's Day: Find out what kind of wine she likes! If mom isn't a wine drinker, make her brunch and serve non-alcoholic mimosas (mix equal amounts of a non-alcoholic Champagne (try Ariel Brut) and the best quality juice you can find!)

Father's Day: Beer anyone?? If your pop prefers liquid wheat, bag the wine idea and buy him a six-pack of his favorite brew. Otherwise, buy his favorite bottle of wine, take him out to dinner, and be prepared to pay a corkage fee.

Independence Day: Despite the popular belief that beer pairs best with barbecue, there are plenty of delicious wines, like Malbec and dry Rosé that pair exceptionally well with foods like burgers, potato salad, baked beans, watermelon, and pasta salad. When served chilled, Rosé wine is a huge crowd pleaser.

Thanksgiving: Ah, the smell of apple pie baking in the oven... here is a holiday that runs the gamut on flavors and textures. I'd choose a full-bodied white wine (like an oaked Chardonnay) to compliment foods like turkey and gravy, or an aromatic Viognier, whose honeysuckle flavor and creamy texture, complements the foods of the season.

As for red wines, I'd serve a unique red wine like Carginan if you want the attention to be on the wine. Carignan exemplifies flavors of spice and yams on its own, which contributes to the wines' pair-ability with foods of the season. Another great choice is a spicy old vine Zinfandel.

Medium-to-full-bodied red wines like Zinfandel, will pair especially well with cranberry sauce and yams.

Oh, and don't forget the Sauternes and Late Harvest Riesling to pair with those pumpkin and apple pies!

Christmas: In my family, Christmas dinner consists of essentially the same foods that are served at Thanksgiving. Foods like mashed potatoes, stuffing, green beans, turkey or meatless protein substitute, yams, cranberry sauce, and black olives all make their way onto the table in some way, shape, or form. Here is a holiday where I think it's totally appropriate to ask your guests to bring their own favorite bottles of wine so you can focus on the meal!

Bridal / Baby Showers: First and foremost, if you are the one hosting a shower make sure that serving alcohol is appropriate. Then, let the time of day determine what type of wine to serve. Champagne is the perfect brunch-style party wine because it can be made into mimosas or served on its own. Light-bodied wines like Moscato and Rosé are perfect mid-day pairing options for appetizers and desserts.

Wedding: Buying wine for lots of people isn't cheap, and it can stressful appeasing to everyone's taste preferences. The good news is that chances of you having to buy wine for a wedding reception are pretty low. Let's imagine, however, that you are the maid of honor or best man at your best friend's wedding and the alcohol is your responsibility.

First, ask the bride if she wants a few special bottles of wine to be served at the bridal party table during the wedding reception. If she does, try and get members of the bridal party to pitch in for the special bottles of wine. *And remember to bring a bottle opener!*

Once you find out how many people have RSVP'd for the wedding reception, it's time to do some math.

One 750 ml bottle is equivalent to five, 5-ounce glasses of wine. You should plan for two drinks per person, over the span of a three-to-four-hour wedding reception, assuming there isn't an established cocktail hour.

To keep it simple, let's assume you are buying wine for 100 guests and serving the standard 5-ounce glass of wine. This would equal 40 bottles of wine, which is a little over 3 cases (12 bottles = 1 case of wine). And, this is probably the only occasion I'd suggest buying wine in bulk.

As mentioned earlier, large production wine is much cheaper per bottle than handcrafted wine. I recommend serving both a red and white wine, regardless of the time of day (most weddings are at least past noon, right?), as this will please a wider variety of palates!

CHAPTER 9

• • • • • •

HOW TO STORE AND TRANSPORT WINE

It was a warm summer day and I had just got home from shopping. My backseat was full of groceries, and heavy ones at that, so I decided to carry as much as I could upstairs and leave the rest in my car until I went out again.

I live on the second floor of a condo complex, so as if carrying heavy groceries upstairs wasn't awkward enough, I also have to balance groceries in one arm while typing a code in for the complex door to open. I rush through the door before it shuts, climb two flights of stairs and often have to set my groceries down to unlock my own door. I generally carry up more than I probably should, to avoid making multiple trips.

So needless to say, I didn't go back to my car until later that evening. Being that it was summer, my car got hot and I forgot that there was a bottle of red wine in my backseat. When I went down to get the rest of my groceries, I saw that the bottle of red wine had leaked everywhere. Ugh. I knew better.

Not only does heat affect the cork, causing it to expand and literally explode, like it did in my case, but exposing wine to heat for long periods of time actually damages the structural components of the wine.

On grocery store shelves, wine is stored standing upright underneath fluorescent lights, in an air-conditioned environment. These conditions are not ideal for long-term storage of wine.

Unopened wine bottles are best stored on their sides in a dark, cool place like a cellar for the best retention of the wine's structural components. Cellar temperatures are kept at about 55°F, humidity is regulated, and exposure to light is minimal.

One of the major purposes of storing wine on its side is to prevent corks from drying out. Dried-out corks start to disintegrate and can crumble when you open the bottle of wine with a corkscrew. One of the benefits of corkless wine bottles is that you won't run into this problem.

Once Wine is Opened

Wine that has been opened and properly sealed, should be stored upright in the fridge and consumed within 3-4 days after opening. Reseal corkless wine bottles simply by putting the screw-off top back on the bottle and use corks to reseal bottles of wine that require cork stoppers. If, however, you mutilated the cork while trying to open the bottle of wine with a cork-screw, you'll want to reseal the bottle with a wine stopper. You should be able to find basic wine stoppers at any home goods store.

Remember that the corks of Champagne bottles expand upon opening, so I highly recommend investing in a Champagne-specific bottle topper to help your wine last longer in the fridge.

Storing wine in the fridge helps slow down chemical processes like oxidation. The more often you open and close a wine bottle, the quicker wine will go flat and lose its flavor. If you're struggling to finish a bottle of wine within three days, don't fret. Wine won't become undrinkable, even after a week of being the fridge. Just don't expect it to taste as fresh as it did the day you opened it!

Aging Wine

Storing wine in a dark, cool place allows the wine to age properly. Wine essentially starts to age once it's bottled, but there are benefits to letting wine sit in a cellar for longer periods of time. The natural acidity in medium-to-light bodied white wines for example, improve their flavor over time. And as mentioned earlier, the tannins in a full-bodied red wine like Cabernet Sauvignon, can soften-- especially after sitting in a cellar for five years.

Sometimes wine changes color during the aging process, which can indicate that wine was exposed to too much oxygen. Pale white wine for example, turns brown when its structural components are damaged by oxidation. Brown wine won't harm you (so I've heard) but the flavor of the wine will be negatively impacted and it'll look gross in your stemware.

Red wine can change color over time as well, but this is not a sign of bad wine. As red wine ages, the tannins soften and red pigments called anthocyanins sometimes give the wine an orangish hue!

Dessert wines like Sauternes, with high residual sugar and relatively low alcohol content, are prime candidates for aging. Generally, the *lower* the alcohol level and the higher the sugar content, the better a wine can age.

Fortified wines are the exception, however, as the added spirits, such as brandy, protect the wine from the volatile effects of alcohol, giving fortified wine a very long shelf life.

You should know, that if you plan to age wine for five or more years, naturally-occurring sediment will most likely cling to the side of the bottle. Sediment is a harmless mixture of dead yeast cells, grape skins and seeds, tartrates, and polymers.

It's suggested that you let the bottle of wine rest upright for a few days before opening, to give the sediment time to drop to the bottom of the bottle. Decanting the wine before drinking it can help reduce sediment in your glass as well--even with wines who haven't been sitting around for five years.

If, however, sediment makes it into your glass (and it often does) be careful washing it out!

When Wine Goes Bad

During my time as a wine educator, it was my responsibility to smell and sample each wine before serving it to my customers. Part of my job was to make sure that opened wine didn't taste like vinegar and that unopened wine hadn't gone bad.

Bottled wine that's been sealed with a cork stopper can be affected by a naturally-occurring compound in wood corks called trichloroacetic acid (TCA).

TCA is non-toxic on its own, but when the compound comes in contact with various other substances like bleach (which is commonly used in wineries for sanitization purposes) it can cause what's called a *cork taint* in wine it can cause what's called a *cork taint* in wine.

Wine that has been corked (affected by TCA) will have strong scents of wet dog, cardboard, and/or a musty attic. If you come across any one of these scents in a New World wine don't drink it. Old World wine, on the other hand, can often have slight aromas of damp mildew, so I'd suggest tasting it before tossing it out. If the wine tastes stale, it is best not to drink it.

More often than not, your wine will be perfectly fine. Of all the bottles of wine that I've opened since 2012, I've only come across three or four bottles of wine affected by cork taint. What happens more frequently, is that I open a bottle of wine for which I just don't have a personal preference for. Fortunately, my husband isn't as picky as I am, so wine rarely ever goes to waste!

Wine in the Car

When traveling with unopened wine in the car--whether it be 20 minutes home from the grocery store or several hours to a friend's place--it's a good idea to put wine in the backseat or trunk of your car. I highly suggest carrying wine in special bags with dividers or wrapped in bubble wrap to protect the wines' integrity.

Being that wine is sensitive to heat and extreme cold, it's important not to freeze your wine or let it sit in the direct sunlight.

Wine that has been opened and re-corked definitely needs to be stored in the trunk of your car, as it is illegal to have open alcoholic beverages in the car's cabin.

Flying with Wine

It's totally legal to put alcohol in your checked-in bag when flying international or domestic. When flying internationally, however, there is a limit to *how much* alcohol you can pack per bag duty free. If returning to the U.S. from an international airport, anything beyond 1 liter of alcohol per person will incur import fees.

When traveling domestic, there is a limit of 5 liters of alcohol between 24%-70% ABV per person in checked luggage. Alcohol beverages with more than 70% ABV are considered a fire hazard and cannot be packed in checked luggage.

Can I Bring Wine to the Park?

On a number of occasions, I've found myself wanting to bring a bottle of wine, a French baguette, and cheese to the park for a picnic. I've gone as far as seeing the whole thing happen in my mind: I'm walking barefoot in the lush green grass with a flowy sundress, turning back and laughing as my long blonde hair blows carelessly in the wind. My man greets me with a handsome smile, a bottle of wine in one hand and two glasses in the other.

Then, almost simultaneously, our eyes fall upon a huge yellow sign stating that no alcohol or glass beverages are allowed in the park. The reality is that parks in the United States are protected by law, restricting things such as open fires, alcohol, and glass beverages.

The good news is that you don't have to go to the park to experience a wine-and-cheese tasting outdoors. Plenty of wineries offer picnic tables and spaces outside for you to enjoy a glass of wine.

And if you have a nice backyard, you could do the whole sunset wine-and-dine thing on a blanket in the grass or make it an elegant evening and bring out the white tablecloth, candles, and fine china. Or, take your wine in a flask, pack some food in a backpack, and picnic in the mountains.

CHAPTER 10

• • • • • •

IS WINE REALLY HEALTHY?

Of all the chapters I've written in this book, I was looking forward to writing this one the most. Being a personal trainer and a lover of wine, I've heard varying degrees of opinions from trainers, the media, and clients relating to alcohol consumption and staying physically fit.

As a trainer, I've advised clients to cut back on alcohol intake and sometimes completely remove it from their diets. But is there a direct correlation between the consumption of alcohol and *weight gain*? If the media is telling everyone that wine is healthy, then why are fitness professionals telling their clients to reduce their consumption of alcohol? In this chapter, I'll address this question by focusing on two ingredients in wine that influence people's health the most: alcohol and sugar.

Social media tells us that wine has the ability to reduce the risk of heart disease by fighting off free radicals and lowering blood pressure.

Several people have told me that their doctor prescribed them a glass of wine in an effort to reduce cardiovascular disease. Unfortunately, the health benefits of wine are gravely misunderstood.

First of all, not *all* wine is created equal when speaking specially to its health value. The health benefits of wine vary by varietal, and not all wines have the same levels of sugar and alcohol.

Red wine is the lowest in sugar compared to most wines, the highest in alcohol, and provides health benefits in the form of antioxidants. White wine tends to be lower in alcohol, higher in sugar, and doesn't provide any health benefits in the form of antioxidants.

I also imagine that most of us don't measure out our wine, but *The Dietary Guidelines for Americans* defines one glass (standard drink) of wine as 5 ounces of 12% ABV wine. This means that for wine to be considered a *healthy practice* you'd be drinking one 5-ounce glass of red wine with a 12% ABV. *And FYI – most red wines in the U.S. are way above 12% ABV!*

The Antioxidants

Red wine contains an organic, plant-based ingredient called resveratrol. Resveratrol is part of a group of compounds called polyphenols which act like antioxidants in the body, preventing damage caused by free radicals.

Free radicals are abnormally charged ions, atoms, or molecules that are produced both naturally and *unnaturally* in the body. Free radicals are also byproducts of eating and breathing.

The number of free radicals floating around in the body increases, when we expose ourselves to air pollutants, cigarette smoke, and industrial chemicals.

An overproduction of free radicals causes varying degrees of problems, ranging from skin damage and inflammatory joint disease to more serious illnesses like cardiovascular diseases and cancer.

The good news is that we can reduce the number of free radicals in our body by controlling our environment *and* by eating a plant-based diet.

Plant-based diets are full of foods that protect against free radicals. Spices and herbs rank as having some of the highest levels of antioxidants, along with foods like cranberries, blueberries, nuts, potatoes, and dark chocolate. And yes, red wine is a source of antioxidants when consumed in moderation.

Did you know? Blue-violet wines like Petite Syrah and Touriga National contain a plant-based compound called anthocyanin, which contributes to many of the health benefits attributed to wine.

Sugar

It exists in *every* bottle of wine.

As mentioned earlier, winemakers can control the level of sugar in wine by managing how much yeast they add to the wine during the fermentation process.

More yeast = more alcohol, and inevitably *less* sugar.

Sugar levels in wine are measured in Brix. Being that wine bottles don't include nutrition labels, there isn't an easy way to find out *exactly* how much sugar is in a particular bottle of wine.

In general, red wines have the least amount of sugar per serving and dessert wines have the most. Here is quick little chart for easy reference:

Lowest	**Low**	**Highest**	**High**
Red wine	Dry Champagne	White wine	Dessert wine

The sugar that exists in wine is natural grape sugar, better known as fructose. When the body starts to digest fructose, it converts the fructose into glucose to be used for immediate energy.

If the body has enough energy (calories) to sustain homeostasis, glucose is stored as glycogen in the liver and muscle tissue. When our immediate energy needs are being met and our glycogen stores are full, excess energy is stored as body fat.

Sugar is a form of carbohydrate, and along with fats and proteins, all three of these macronutrients can be stored as body fat when consumed in excess. The more wine you drink in one sitting, the more sugar your body needs to digest and store. Even wine that is relatively low in sugar should be consumed in moderation, especially if it's high in alcohol.

Did you know? Most non-alcoholic sparkling beverages contain ***more*** sugar per 5-ounce serving than red or white wine.

Alcohol

You might find it interesting to know that alcohol is *never* stored as energy (glycogen) in the body. This means that when you eat food with your wine, the food is not the preferred source of immediate energy. The body will use the calories in ethanol first and store nutrients consumed from food as glycogen. My telling you this, is by *NO* means a ploy to try and get you to consume alcohol without food. The body needs food to help absorb the ethanol in alcoholic beverages. Rather, the focus should be on your *overall* daily intake of calories.

The Dietary Guidelines for Americans recommends that women limit their consumption of alcohol to one standard drink per day, and men limit their consumption of alcohol to two standard drinks per day.

So why are there different recommendations for women and men?

Well, first of all, men have high levels of an enzyme called alcohol dehydrogenase (ADH) in their stomach and liver. ADH is the primary enzyme responsible for metabolizing alcohol. Women, don't have *any* ADH in their stomach and very low levels of the enzyme in their liver. The liver can only metabolize about 15 grams of ethanol per hour, which, you can probably guess, is equivalent to **one** 12-ounce beer or **one** 5-ounce glass of 12% ABV wine.

If alcohol is consumed beyond what the liver can metabolize per hour, the excess alcohol gets directly delivered to the blood stream, which increases your blood alcohol concentration (BAC) levels. Blood alcohol concentration is a measurement of alcohol intoxication.

The speed at which BAC levels rise is directly related to the volume of alcohol consumed within a particular time frame, as well as how hydrated you are.

Men have more muscle tissue compared to women, and muscle tissue contains more water than fat. Alcohol requires water from within the body to metabolize. As BAC levels rise so does the need for water. The more alcohol you drink, the quicker you'll become dehydrated (and intoxicated) if you aren't drinking enough water to stay hydrated.

Women especially need to be attentive to how much water they drink while consuming alcohol!

Most of us know that eating food slows down the rate at which alcohol is absorbed into our digestive system. Research has been done, correlating drinking alcohol with an increase in consumption of foods that are high in fat and sodium. Certain parts of the brain responsible for sensing hunger are dampened with the consumption of alcohol.

I suggest making intentional choices <u>before</u> you start drinking, like predetermining the size of your meal and limiting the availability of foods high in fat and sodium.

The recipes in the following chapter are designed to not only to pair well with wine, but also to contribute to your overall health and wellness. Of course, certain foods like pizza and shortbread are meant to be enjoyed on occasion! ☺

CHAPTER 11

• • • • • • •

PLANT-BASED RECIPES AND WINE PAIRINGS

I'm excited to share the following recipes with you because they are all vegetarian and make fantastic pairing-partners to a wide variety of wines.

For the purpose of this book, we are defining *plant-based* as a way of eating that focuses on lots of vegetables, whole grains, nuts, seeds, and legumes with very few meat or dairy products.

The goal of this book is to provide you with relatively healthy and meatless meal options that pair well with wine. You'll find that most of the recipes are fairly simple, but I've included several recipes (like pizza) which require a bit more time. I promise they are well worth the wait!

Most of the recipes include both an Old and New World wine-pairing option, with an explanation of why I chose that particular wine to pair with the dish.

I had fun developing these recipes, with a few being direct requests from friends and readers like you.

Appetizers. Dips. Salads

Honeyed Goat Cheese Bruschetta with Fresh Peaches and Basil

Serves 6 (2 slices per person)

I serve this bruschetta with mimosas for breakfast when company is over! The bruschetta is easy to assemble and pairs beautifully with a fruity sparkling beverage (Martinelli's is a great non-alcoholic option!)

---

1 baguette French bread
1 tube honeyed goat cheese
1-2 fresh peaches, peeled & sliced
1 bunch fresh basil, washed & freshly chopped

Preheat oven to 350°F. Slice baguette diagonally and place on ungreased cookie sheet. Toast bread for 5 minutes, then flip over and toast for another 5 minutes until golden brown on both sides. Cool slightly, then spread goat cheese on warm bread. Top with freshly-sliced peaches and chopped basil.

Pairs best with: Champagne
The tiny bubbles of Champagne create an effervescence that cuts through the oils and saltiness of cheese.
New World option: Mumm Brut, Napa Valley
Old World option: Pierre Moncuit Delos Grand Cru Blanc de Blancs, France

Alternative wine pairing: Sparkling wine
Italian Prosecco – extra dry
Spanish Cava – extra dry
German or Austrian Sekt – dry or off-dry
French Cremant – dryness can vary

Simple Mimosa Recipe

Mix equals parts of Champagne and your choice of juice in a flute glass. Cheers!

Cheese, Fruit, and Nut Platter

Serves 4-6

I recommend using a combination of soft and hard cheeses with a variety of crackers, nuts, and dried fruit. Offering a variety of jams and savory chutneys is a lovely pairing-option as well.

1-2 soft cheeses (I like Brie and Fontina)
1-2 hard cheeses (Gruyere, Colby, Cheddar, and/or Monterey Jack)*
Assortment of nuts (cashews, almonds, walnuts, pecans)
Dried and/or fresh fruit
Assortment of crackers

Lay all your ingredients out on a cheese or cutting board just before serving. Be sure to lay out small plates, napkins, and utensils for cutting and spreading the cheese.

Optional: jams, chutneys, compotes, flavored honey

*Feel free to substitute your favorite vegan hard-style cheeses to suite your tastes!

Pairs best with: Champagne
Champagne's high acidity offsets the saltiness of the nuts and complements the natural acidity in fresh and dried fruits.

White Bean Dip with Crostini

Makes 2 1/2 cups

One of my favorite dips to bring to parties! This dip is healthy, creamy, light, and citrusy. Serve with crostini, raw vegetables, and fresh pita.

1-2 garlic cloves
2 (15-ounce) cans of white beans (navy or cannellini), rinsed & drained
1 cup fresh parsley, de-stemmed and packed tight
2-3 Tbsp fresh lemon juice
3/4 tsp each salt
1/2 tsp freshly ground black pepper
3 Tbsp extra virgin olive oil
1 Tbsp water

Pulse garlic in a food processor until minced. Add beans, parsley, juice, salt, and pepper – process until smooth. With processor on, slowly add oil and water through food chute. Stop and scrape down sides and continue processing until desired consistency is achieved.

Pairs best with: Albarino
A not-so mainstream gem of the white wine world. This delightful citrusy wine from Spain can be found at most fine wine retailers.
Old World option: Val Do Sosego Albarino, Rias Baixas

Creamy Caesar Salad

Serves 6

I have been asked multiple times for this anchovy-free salad dressing but haven't decided to share it until now! It is super creamy and can double as a dip for vegetables. Feel free to add chicken if you eat meat or omit the cheese to make it vegan!

Dressing (makes 3/4 cup)
1 garlic clove
3/4 cup Original Vegenaise
1 Tbsp red wine vinegar
1 tsp vegan Worcestershire sauce
1 tsp mustard
Pinch of black pepper, plus more to taste

Process one clove of garlic in a medium-sized food processer. Add the Vegenaise, red wine vinegar, Worcestershire sauce, mustard, and freshly ground pepper. Process until smooth and blended. Adjust consistency and taste by adding more of any ingredient.

Salad
1-2 heads of romaine lettuce
Freshly grated Parmesan cheese
Croutons (*see recipe below for homemade version!)*

Wash and spin the lettuce and tear or chop into a big bowl. Layer the lettuce and freshly grated Parmesan cheese (if using). Serve the croutons and dressing on the side.

Pairs best with: Chenin Blanc & Viognier Blend
Any dry, crisp, aromatic medium-to-light-bodied white wine will pair well with this rich, creamy salad.
New World option: Pine Ridge Chenin Blanc + Vioginer Blend 2016, Napa

Homemade Croutons

I learned how to make croutons while working at a bakery in college. Making your own croutons is a super easy way to use up bread that's gone dry, with no added preservatives!

You can use any kind of day-old bread.

Preheat oven to 350°F. Cut bread into dice-sized cubes (or however big you like your croutons) and place on ungreased cookie sheet. Bake for 15-20 minutes or until lightly golden brown. Check on the croutons when you start to smell them.

Smashed Red Potatoes with Parsley 'n Walnut Pesto

Serves 4 (2 potatoes per person)

This is a simple side dish that also makes great leftovers. Potatoes are boiled and then smashed and roasted to an undeniably crispy texture that's worth the effort.

----

8 small organic red potatoes, washed & scrubbed with peels left on
Extra virgin olive oil
1/4 tsp each salt and black pepper, plus more to taste
Coconut oil spray

Parsley Walnut Pesto (*see recipe for roasted vegetables)*

Preheat oven to 475°F. Place potatoes in a large pot of water and bring to a boil over high heat. Let potatoes remain at a boil, slightly covering the pot with a lid for about 18-20 minutes. Run a fork through several potatoes to determine if potatoes are done. Remove from heat, then drain and let cool. Once the potatoes have cooled, place them on a large, greased cookie sheet. Using a pot holder or towel, lightly smash each potato.

Brush smashed potatoes with enough olive oil to coat the tops. Sprinkle with salt and pepper, then place in preheated oven. Let potatoes bake for 30 minutes until crispy golden brown and remove from oven. Serve potatoes with parsley walnut pesto, or brush with more olive oil, and serve with salt and pepper.

Pairs best with: Sauvignon Blanc
Crisp, fresh, and acidic Sauvignon Blanc complements the lemon-parsley sauce and starchy potatoes.
New World option: Honig Rutherford Reserve Sauvignon Blanc 2014, Napa
Old World option: Bernier Sauvignon Blanc 2013, France

Brussels Sprouts with Balsamic Reduction

Serves 4-6

Spruce up your steamed sprouts with a sweet and tangy balsamic sauce!

---

6 cups of Brussels sprouts, halved
1 cup balsamic vinegar (the best quality)
1 Tbsp pure maple syrup or honey
1/4 tsp each salt and black pepper, plus more to taste

Remove any loose outer leaves from the Brussels sprouts and slice in half. Place the sprouts evenly in a large sauté pan and fill halfway with water (enough to cook the sprouts without completely covering).

Bring to a boil over high heat. Reduce heat to low and cover with lid slightly cocked. Cook for 10-15 minutes then drain.

Place the balsamic vinegar and sweetener in a small saucepan and bring to a boil. Reduce heat to medium-low and cook for about 10-15 minutes, stirring frequently to prevent the vinegar from sticking to the pan.

As the vinegar starts to reduce in volume, check periodically for desired thickness by dipping the back end of a spoon into the sauce. The vinegar reduction is done when it coats the back of a spoon.

Drizzle balsamic reduction over warm Brussels sprouts and serve with salt and pepper.

Pairs best with: Merlot
A good-quality, fruity balsamic vinegar will match the dark fruit flavors of a full-bodied red wine like Merlot.
New World option: Trefethen Merlot 2014, Napa
Old World option: Luc Pirlet Reserve Merlot, France

Meatless Main Dishes

Black Bean Sliders and Sweet Potato Fries

Serves 2-4 (will vary depending on size of patty and how many fries you make)

These black bean burgers can easily be shaped into regular-sized burger patties or slider-sized portions. Slider-sized burger patties work best for *protein-style*, which simply means to serve it without a bun. The sweet potato fries are roasted rather than fried and are delicious on their own or dipped in a combo of mayo and hot sauce.

---

1 (15-ounce) can black beans, rinsed & drained
1/4 cup red onion, finely chopped
1 tsp cumin
1/4 tsp each salt and black pepper, plus more to taste
1/2 cup cracker crumbs (sub regular or GF oat flour, if desired)
1 egg or egg replacer
Fresh 'n Crisp leaves of lettuce (to use as a wrap like shown in photo)*
Nonstick cooking spray (I use coconut oil spray)

Optional: tomatoes, avocado, onion, mayo, mustard, cheddar

Mash black beans in a large bowl with potato masher. Mix in onion, cumin, salt, pepper, cracker crumbs (or oat flour), and egg. Shape into patties, according to desired size. Fry patties in a lightly-greased skillet on medium-high heat until brown and crispy on both sides.

If using cheese: Top patties with cheese while they are still in the skillet (put a lid on top if necessary to melt the cheese faster).

Assembly: Spread condiments on a large, crisp leaf of lettuce. Add the patty and stack with tomatoes, onions, avocado, and whatever else you like. *Just don't get too crazy with your fixin's, as you have to wrap the lettuce around everything!*

Sweet Potato Fries

2 yams (the orange-skinned sweet potatoes), peeled & cut into strips - *makes about 4 servings*
2 Tbsp avocado oil
1/2 tsp garlic powder
1/2 tsp chili powder
1/2 tsp paprika
1/2 tsp onion salt
1/4 tsp ground red pepper
1/4 tsp turmeric (optional)

Preheat oven to 450°F. Peel and cut potatoes into strips and place in roasting pan.

Drizzle potatoes with the avocado oil, then mix in the spices. (If you don't have a roasting pan, grease one large- rimmed baking sheet and mix the potatoes with the oil and spices in a separate large bowl.) Spread the potato strips evenly in the pan, and place in the oven.

Bake for 20-30 minutes. Use oven-safe spatula to carefully move fries around in the pan every so often to check for doneness.

Pairs best with: Valpolicella
The earthy characteristics of this juicy red wine pairs harmoniously with the earthy flavor of black beans.

Old World option: Rafael Valpolicella Classico Superiore 2013, Italy *(Avoid Amarone and Recioto style for the purpose of this pairing).*

Alternative wine pairings: Zinfandel, Shiraz, Tempranillo
Pick a medium-to-full-bodied red wine with good fruit and spice to complement the spicy sweet potato fries and offset the earthy black bean burgers.

P.S. Shiraz is Australia's Syrah grape. Different growing region = very different flavor! Try it!

Mushroom Lentil Burgers

Makes 12-13 regular-sized patties

These patties are vegan, high in protein, and can easily be made gluten-free. The arugula and not-so-special sauce adds a unique flavor, but mustard and mayo would work just fine.

1/8 cup (2 Tbsp) avocado oil
1 small onion, diced
3 garlic cloves, minced
4 cups fresh mushrooms, sliced
3 cups brown lentils, precooked (1 cup uncooked = 3 cups cooked)
1/2 tsp salt
1/4 tsp marjoram
1/4 tsp freshly ground black pepper
1/2 tsp cumin
1 flaxseed egg (1 Tbsp flaxmeal + 2 1/2 Tbsp water)
2/3 cup ground walnuts
1 cup oat flour (GF oat flour works as well)
1 cup bread crumbs (I tossed one of the hamburger buns in my food processor)
Hamburger buns
Arugula
Tomatoes
Onion

Heat avocado oil in a large sauté pan over medium-high heat. Add onion and garlic and sauté for about 6-8 minutes until translucent. Add sliced mushrooms and sauté until most of the liquid is absorbed, about 8-10 minutes.

Remove pan from heat to let mushroom mixture cool. Place precooked lentils in a large food processor, then add mushroom mixture and seasonings. Pulse ingredients several times just until blended, while keeping some texture in the mixture. In a large bowl, mix the flaxseed egg and let thicken for about 3-5 minutes before mixing with other ingredients.

When ready, transfer mushroom mixture to the large bowl and add ground walnuts. Stir in oat flour and breadcrumbs. Heat skillet over medium-high heat and grease with olive oil or coconut oil spray. Use the palm of your hand to shape dough into patties. Place patties in the hot skillet and cook until golden brown on both sides, about 4-6 minutes.

Once cooked, transfer patties to plate or wire cooling rack. Layer the arugula, tomato, onion, and sauce as shown the photo below.

Not-So Secret Sauce

1/2 cup Vegenaise (or sub regular mayo)
2 Tbsp Tapatio (or Cholula)

Whisk ingredients until blended. Spoon on top of burger patties.

Pairs best with: Syrah
Warmer climate Syrah, like the one I am featuring here from the Sierra Foothills, is fruity and spicy, with notes of leather, and sweet tobacco. Full-bodied red wines like Syrah, pair really well with earthy-flavored foods like mushrooms and lentils.
New World option: Wise Villa Winery Syrah 2012, Sierra Foothills

Classic Pizza Margarita

Makes 2 crusts

I have to give credit to my mother-in-law for giving me this recipe. No kneading or punching down dough--just some waiting time--to make this delicious pizza crust.

----

3 1/2 cups lukewarm water (100°F)
1 Tbsp yeast
1 Tbsp kosher salt
7 1/2 cups all-purpose white flour

Marinara sauce (*recipe below*)
Sliced fresh tomatoes, deseeded
Fresh basil, chopped
Fresh mozzarella, sliced with a serrated knife

**Pizza dough notes*: I found that the pliability of the dough is best when the dough has been in the fridge for at least 8 hours.

Measure and pour the flour into a large bowl. Add yeast and salt to lukewarm water, then mix into bowl of flour. Cover with lid or Saran Wrap and let rise at room temperature for 2 hours (don't punch down dough). Once dough has risen, let the dough rest in fridge for a minimum of 3 hours before baking. *Dough will stay good in the fridge (covered) for 3-5 days.

Place a pizza stone in the oven. Preheat the oven to 475°F, allowing the stone to get hot.

Roll out the pizza dough on a floured surface until it is approximately 8 to 10-inches round and 1/4-inch thick. Place the pizza dough on a large piece of parchment paper, ideally on a pizza peel. Ladle the sauce onto the dough, leaving about a 1-inch border around the edge.

Top with fresh mozzarella and place pizza dough with parchment paper onto the hot pizza stone. Bake until crust is golden and the cheese has melted, about 15-20 minutes. Top with freshly sliced tomatoes and chopped fresh basil. Cut into wedges and serve immediately.

Pairs best with: Sangiovese
Being Italy's most widely-planted grape, it's no wonder Sangiovese pairs so well with flavors like tomatoes, basil, and fresh cheese.

New World option: Wise Villa Winery Sangiovese, Sierra Foothills
Old World option: Chianti Classico, Italy

Red Wine Marinara Sauce

Makes 4 1/2 cups

I use this sauce for pizza *and* spaghetti! The tomato paste in this recipe helps thicken the sauce, but this recipe can be made without it.

1 Tbsp avocado oil
1/2 large onion, finely chopped
2 garlic cloves, minced
1/8 cup quality red wine (such as Zinfandel or Chianti)
1 (28-ounce) can crushed tomatoes
1 (14-ounce) can diced tomatoes
1-2 Tbsp tomato paste
1 tsp dried basil
1 tsp dried oregano
2 tsp sugar
1/2 tsp salt
1/4 tsp freshly ground black pepper

In a large sauté pan, heat oil over medium heat. Add onion and garlic, and sauté for 5-8 minutes or until the onions are translucent and lightly-browned. Add red wine and sauté until most of the liquid is absorbed, about 2-3 minutes. Add crushed tomatoes, diced tomatoes, tomato paste, basil, oregano, sugar, salt, and pepper. Bring to a boil. Reduce heat to low, cover and simmer for 15-20 minutes, stirring occasionally.

Cauliflower and Potato Curry

Serves 8 (1-cup servings)

Serve this delicious (and not too spicy) curry over jasmine or basmati rice, with naan, or on its own.

----

2 Tbsp avocado oil
1 large onion, chopped
3 garlic cloves, minced
1/4 tsp ground ginger
1/2 tsp turmeric
1 tsp cumin
1 tsp curry powder
1 (14-ounce) can diced tomatoes
1 (14-ounce) can stewed tomatoes, chopped
1 cup vegetarian broth
1 tsp sugar
1 head of cauliflower, cut into florets
2 golden potatoes, peeled & cubed
1/2 tsp salt, plus more to taste
Squeeze of lemon juice
Rice
Naan

Heat oil over medium-low heat in a large pot. Cook onion until soft, around 5-10 minutes. Then add garlic, ginger, turmeric, cumin, and curry powder. Cook for 1 minute. Stir in tomatoes, 1/2 cup broth, and sugar. Add the cauliflower, potatoes, and salt then cover with a lid. Gently cook curry for 30-45 minutes, stirring occasionally, until the vegetables are tender. Add more broth if curry is too thick. Squeeze fresh lemon juice over curry and serve with rice or naan.

Pairs best with: Riesling
Fruit-forward Rieslings with high acidity, balance out the spicy nature of flavorful dishes like curry.
New World option: Trefethen Dry Riesling 2016, Napa
Old World option: Dr. L Riesling, Germany

Greek Salad Wrap

Serves 5 (if using all the wraps available in one package)

The perfect meal when you are dining solo or serving a crowd. These wraps are easy to make, and best served with a simple, light white wine or rosé.

----

1 package of Lavash bread (rectangular flatbread)
1 package of mixed greens (or wash & chop your own lettuce mix)
Kalamata olives, sliced or chopped
Tomatoes, chopped
Avocado, cubed
Bell Pepper, chopped
Salt & pepper to taste
The Best Hummus (*recipe below*)
Balsamic Vinaigrette (*recipe below)*

Warm flatbread in the microwave or in a lightly greased skillet, just before serving. Spread a layer of hummus on the warmed Lavash bread. Top with mixed greens, olives, tomatoes, avocado, bell pepper, salt, and pepper. Drizzle the balsamic vinaigrette over the mixed greens and roll into a burrito.

Pairs best with: Vinho Verde
Crisp and refreshing, this pale green wine delivers fresh flavors of lemon and grapefruit, with welcome notes of basil and minerals. White wines like Vinho Verde with high acidity and low alcohol, match the acidity in vinaigrette dressings and compliment the briny Kalamata olives.
Old World option: Aveleda Vinho Verde 2016, Portugal

The Best Hummus

Makes 2 1/2 cups

This hummus is super simple to make and undoubtedly, my favorite go-to dip for parties!

----

2 garlic cloves
2 (15 ½-ounce) cans garbanzo beans (chickpeas), drained & rinsed
1/4 cup fresh lemon juice
1/4 cup tahini (remember to stir the tahini if you are opening a new jar!)
2 Tbsp water
3/4 tsp salt
1/2 tsp freshly ground black pepper
4-5 Tbsp extra virgin olive oil (*see "How to Choose the Best Olive Oil" on pg. 110*)

Pulse garlic in large food processor until completely chopped. Add the garbanzo beans (chickpeas), lemon juice, tahini, water, salt, and pepper. With the food processor running, add the extra virgin olive oil through the food chute. Stop and scrap down the sides periodically and continue to blend until desired consistency is reached.

Place hummus in bowl and serve with pita bread or vegetables.

Hummus freezes well. Be sure to thaw at least 24-48 hours in the refrigerator before use.

Balsamic Vinaigrette

Homemade dressing is delicious and much healthier than store-bought dressings. Choose any fruity vinegar and quality olive oil and mix a 3:1 ratio of olive oil to vinegar – add some salt and pepper and BOOM, you've got yourself a salad dressing!

3/4 cup extra virgin olive oil
1/4 cup balsamic vinegar
Salt and pepper to taste

Wisk together olive oil and vinegar until emulsified, just before serving. Dressing stays fresh in the refrigerator for one week.

Roasted Vegetables with Parsley Walnut Pesto

Serves 2-3 (as a main dish)

For the best flavor, choose vegetables that are in season and serve the roasted vegetables over rice or pasta. Toss in some cubed tofu for protein or add cooked chicken if you eat meat.

Vegetable Options:
1 cup baby carrots, sliced in half
1 cup broccoli florets
1 cup cauliflower florets
1 cup mushrooms, cut in half or quartered (depending on size)
1 cup zucchini or yellow squash, cubed or sliced into thick pieces
1 cup butternut squash, cubed
1 cup parsnips, cubed or sliced into thick pieces
1 cup onion (red or white) cubed
1/4 tsp each salt and pepper, plus more to taste

Oils:
1/4 cup avocado oil (for roasting)
Drizzle of extra virgin olive oil (for the finish)

Protein Options:
Cubed tofu (roast with vegetables)
White beans, rinsed & drained (serve on top of roasted vegetables)
Cooked meat of choice

Carbohydrate Options:
Pasta (wheat, white, gluten-free)
Rice (brown, white, jasmine, basmati)

Parsley Walnut Pesto (*recipe below*)

Preheat oven to 475°F. Chop vegetables into relatively even pieces and toss with a 1/4 cup of avocado oil in a large bowl or directly in the roasting pan. Add salt & pepper and toss in cubed tofu (if using).

Roast for 30 minutes or until nicely browned and a fork glides easily through the vegetables. While vegetables are roasting, cook the pasta or rice and make parsley walnut pesto.

Place cooked rice or pasta in individual bowls, then add pesto, vegetables, and protein. Top with white beans. Drizzle with extra virgin olive oil if desired, and season with more salt and pepper.

Pairs best with: Chardonnay
The rich toasty flavors of a Chardonnay complement the nutty pesto, earthy white beans, and roasted vegetables.
New World option: Hess Collection Chardonnay 2013, Monterey.
Old World option: Luisi Chardonnay, Italy

Alternative wine pairing: Pinot Noir
Pinot Noir is a food-friendly wine, due to its bright acidity and relatively low alcohol content. I pair it with this dish to offset the earthy vegetables and complement the savory pesto.

MERLOT & BRUSSELS SPROUTS

Parsley Walnut Pesto

Makes 1 cup

Parsley is an excellent source of vitamin K - a key fat-soluble vitamin responsible for blood-clotting. Not only is parsley healthy for you, but it's widely available at most grocery stores. This pesto is delicious mixed into rice and served with roasted vegetables as pictured here, or served on top of smashed red potatoes.

---

1 garlic clove
1 cup walnut halves
4 cups fresh parsley, rinsed & destemmed
2 Tbsp fresh lemon juice
1/2 tsp salt
1/4 tsp freshly ground black pepper
1/3 cup extra virgin olive oil

Pulse garlic in large food processor until completely chopped. Add the walnuts, parsley, lemon juice, salt, and pepper. Scrape down sides. With the food processor running, add the extra virgin olive oil until desired consistency is reached.

*If pesto is too thick, add extra virgin olive oil or water to thin as needed.

Mandy's Vegetarian Chili

Serves 6-8 (1-cup servings)

I was making this chili for years without a recipe, until I was asked by a friend if I'd be willing to share "the recipe." Hope you enjoy it as much as I do, and feel free to add or subtract any of the vegetables to suit your taste!

1-2 Tbsp avocado oil
1 small white onion, finely chopped
2 garlic cloves, minced
1-2 zucchini, chopped
1 bell pepper, chopped
2-3 stalks of celery, chopped
1-2 large carrots, peeled & finely chopped
1 Tbsp chili powder
1 Tbsp cumin
1 tsp oregano
1 (14-ounce) can diced tomatoes
1 Tbsp tomato paste
1 (8-ounce) can tomato sauce (optional)
1 cup corn, frozen or canned
1 (15-ounce) can pinto beans, drained & rinsed
1 (15-ounce) can kidney beans, drained & rinsed
1 (15-ounce) can black beans, drained & rinsed
1 (32-ounce) carton of veggie broth
1 tsp salt
1/2 tsp freshly ground pepper

Heat a large soup pot over medium heat. Once pot is warmed, add avocado oil and chopped vegetables (onion through carrot). Add seasonings and sauté for about 10 minutes (until the veggies are soft). Add diced tomatoes, tomato paste, tomato sauce (if using,) corn, beans, broth, salt, and pepper. Cover and let simmer for 15-20 minutes on medium-to-low heat. Taste-test the chili and adjust cooking time or seasonings accordingly.

Optional: shredded cheese, avocado, sliced black olives, and sour cream for topping.

Pairs best with: Dry Rosé
A chilled dry Rose with high acidity and flavors of fresh fruit pairs surprisingly well with the contrasting flavors and spices of a homey dish like chili.
New World option: Maipe Malbec Rosé, Argentina
Old World option: Aix Rosé Provence 2017, France

Mushroom Risotto

Serves 3-4 (as a main dish)

My risotto rarely comes out looking white. The vegetable broth gives this dish an intriguing, orange-brown hue that actually makes a perfect base for the rustic mushrooms!

6-8 cups vegetable broth
2 Tbsp avocado oil
2 shallots, finely chopped
2 garlic cloves, minced
2 1/2 cups mushrooms, sliced
1/2 cup dry white wine (such as Muscadet, Pinot Grigo, Sauvignon Blanc)
1 1/2 cups Arborio rice (uncooked)
1 tsp salt
1/2 tsp pepper

Pour broth into medium saucepan and keep warm over low heat. In a large sauté pan, heat 2 Tbsp of oil over medium-high heat. Add shallots, garlic, and mushrooms. Sauté for about 5 minutes.

Add rice to mushroom mixture in the sauté pan and cook for about 2 minutes, until the rice looks opaque. Stir in dry white wine and cook until wine is fully absorbed.

Slowly add the broth (one cup at a time) to rice and mushroom mixture, allowing the broth to absorb into the rice before adding more. Continue this process until the rice is just cooked and slightly chewy. You're looking at a 25-30-minute process here, so give yourself time. *Don't add the broth all at once or the rice will not cook properly!* Stir in the salt and pepper and serve!

Pairs best with: Barbera
A full-bodied red wine like Barbera compliments the richness of a dish like mushroom risotto.
New World option: Andis Estate Barbera 2014, Amador County
Old World option: Pelissero Barbera d'Alba Piani 2009, Italy

Orange Tofu with Grilled Peppers & Jasmine Rice

Serves 4 (1/2 cup rice, 1/2 cup pepper sauté, 1 piece of tofu)

I prefer to use gluten-free, non-GMO Bragg Liquid Aminos in this recipe as a substitute for soy sauce.

Tofu:
1 block extra-firm tofu, pressed and cut into 4 pieces
Coconut Spray or olive oil

Orange Glaze:
1/2 cup fresh orange juice (one orange = approx. 1/2 cup)
1 garlic clove, minced
1/4 cup honey
1/4 cup Bragg Liquid Aminos

Bell Pepper Sauté:
1-2 Tbsp avocado oil
1 red bell pepper, sliced
1 green bell pepper, sliced
1 yellow or orange pepper, sliced
Salt and pepper to taste
Crushed red pepper flakes, to taste

Jasmine Rice Pilaf ingredients:
1 cup jasmine rice, uncooked
2 cups vegetable broth (or water if you don't have broth)

How to prepare tofu: Cut tofu in half and place on paper towels between two weighted blocks. Let tofu press for 30 minutes and cut the two halves in half again, for a total of 4 pieces. Heat a large sauté pan over medium-high heat. Add just enough oil or coconut spray to coat the pan. Fry tofu until brown on both sides (adding more olive oil if necessary, to keep tofu from sticking to the pan). Once tofu is heated through, remove pan from heat.

Making the orange glaze: Bring orange juice to a boil in a small saucepan. Reduce heat to medium-high and allow the juice to cook until reduced by half, about 4-5 minutes. Add the garlic, honey, and soy sauce and cook until thickened, about 3-5 minutes. Using a pastry brush, quickly bask the tofu with the orange glaze while pouring sauce into the pan. Sauce will thicken when it cools.

Serve tofu over jasmine rice with sautéed bell peppers or other cooked vegetable.

Making the bell pepper sauté: Heat 1 Tbsp of avocado oil in a large skillet over medium-high heat. Once oil is hot, add the sliced bell pepper. Sauté pepper until tender, adding more oil if necessary (up to 1 Tbsp) to keep the vegetables from sticking to the pan. Cover pan with lid slightly cocked, to speed up the cooking process. Season with salt and pepper.

Making the rice: Place jasmine rice and broth in a medium saucepan and bring to a boil. Cover and reduce heat to low and cook for 15 minutes. Fluff with a fork and serve with tofu and bell pepper sauté.

Pairs best with: Dry White Wine
Delicate white wines with a slight effervescent quality, couple well with foods of varying flavors and textures.
Old World option: Orvieto Classico 2015, Italy

Chickpea & Parsley Falafel

Makes 12 falafel patties

I like to serve my falafel patties on pita bread with ***The Best Hummus*** (recipe under Greek Salad Wrap, pg. 93) or with the garlic dill sauce included in this recipe. Feel free to adjust the seasonings to taste!

Falafel
2-3 garlic cloves
1 (15-ounce) can garbanzo beans (chickpeas), drained & rinsed
1/2 cup packed fresh parsley, destemmed & chopped
1/2 large onion, finely chopped
2 tsp cumin
1 tsp coriander
1/4 tsp each salt and black pepper
4-6 Tbsp of oat flour (or gluten free flour blend)
1-2 Tbsp avocado oil for cooking (or other neutral oil, like grapeseed oil)

Pulse garlic in a large food processor until minced. Add in chickpeas, parsley, onion, and spices. Process until thoroughly mixed but with some texture. Transfer mixture to a large bowl and mix in flour until the dough is moldable.

Cover and refrigerate for 1-2 hours to let dough firm up. Heat a large skillet over medium heat and add enough oil to coat the pan.

While the skillet is heating, carefully shape the falafel dough into patties and add to the preheated skillet.

Cook patties until crispy brown about 4-5 minutes, then carefully flip to cook on the other side. Place patties on parchment-lined cookie sheet and bake 12-14 minutes, flipping over half way through baking time, to bake evenly on both sides. Cool on wire rack.

Garlic dill sauce

1 6-ounce container of plain Greek yogurt
1/2 cup cucumber peeled, seeded, and finely chopped
1 garlic clove, minced
2 Tbsp fresh dill (or 1 tsp dried)
2 tsp fresh lemon juice
1/4 tsp salt

Mix together all ingredients and serve.

Pairs best with: Pinot Grigo
Pinot Grigio and Pinot Gris are the same grape but known by two different names depending on where it's grown. Pinot Gris from the Alsace region of France delivers rich flavors of apple, peach, and minerals. While the Pinot Grigo from Veneto, Italy presents fresh apple and pear aromas with a crisp finish of peach and elderflower.
Old World option: Belvino Pinot Grigio, Italy
Old World option: Albrecht Pinot Gris Tradition, France

Desserts

Apple Pie Crostada

Makes 2 Crostadas

Serve with vanilla bean gelato for dessert, or with coffee for breakfast (my favorite!)

3lbs. apples (or about 7 medium apples = 11 cups), peeled, cored, & sliced
1/4 cup fresh lemon juice
1/2 cup brown sugar (coconut sugar works well too!)
2 Tbsp cornstarch
1/2 tsp ground cinnamon
1/4 tsp allspice
1/2 tsp salt
1 Tbsp cold butter (use at end of assembly)

Filling directions:
Mix sugar, cornstarch, cinnamon, allspice, and salt in a bowl. Add sliced apples and toss to coat evenly.

Crust Ingredients
3 cups all-purpose white flour
1 tsp salt
1 1/4 cups butter, softened
1 egg
1 Tbsp distilled white vinegar
2-5 Tbsp ice water

Equipment
Parchment Paper
Square cookie sheet

Dough directions

Mix flour and salt with whisk in a large bowl. Using a pastry blender, cut butter into flour mixture to form coarse meal. Whisk together egg, vinegar, and **2 Tbsp** ice water in small bowl. Drizzle liquid into the flour mixture, stirring to form dough. If dough is too dry, add 1 Tbsp of water at a time, until dough sticks together.

Cover and refrigerate dough for at least 30 minutes before using. Divide dough in half and form into 2 balls. Flatten into two thick disks and **Refrigerate dough for at least 30 minutes before using.**

Preheat oven to 350°F. Roll one disc out on floured counter into a large circle, approximately 11-inches thick.

Crostada directions

Place dough onto a large, square cookie sheet lined with parchment paper. Spoon half of the apple filling into center of dough, leaving an inch the edge.

Cut 1 tablespoon of butter into small pieces and sprinkle on top of apple filling. Fold edges of dough over apple filling. Place crostada in preheated oven for 50 minutes, until filling is bubbling and the crust is a golden brown.

If making two crostadas, bake one at a time. Filling can be refrigerated and used for a later use, but I'd recommended using within 3-4 days.

Pairs best with: Late Harvest Riesling
A medium-bodied dessert wine with complimentary flavors of tangerine and honey emphasize the natural sweetness of fruit-based desserts.
Old World option: Hogue Late Harvest Riesling 2016, Columbia Valley

Maple Walnut Shortbread Cookies

Makes about 16 cookies

Buttery and crumbly, these cookies melt in your mouth! Sift a little powdered sugar on top to make them look pretty. But seriously… they won't last that long!

3/4 cup organic butter, softened
3 Tbsp pure maple syrup
3/4 tsp pure vanilla extract
1 3/4 all-purpose white flour, sifted
1/4 tsp baking powder
1/8 tsp baking soda
1/2 tsp salt
1/2 cup walnuts, ground (save some whole ones for tops of cookies)

Preheat oven to 350°F. Place softened butter in a large bowl. Mix in vanilla extract and maple syrup. If using an electric mixer, place on low speed and gradually add in flour, baking powder, baking soda, and salt. Stir in ground walnuts by hand. The dough should stick together but be slightly crumbly.

Using a cookie scoop, drop dough onto parchment-lined cookie sheet, about 1-2 inches apart. Flatten cookie dough with palm of hand and place a walnut halve in the center. Bake in a 350°F oven for 12-15 minutes. Let cool and try only eating one!

Pairs best with: Moscato
Fruity flavors of nectarine and peach compliment the nutty shortbread, creating a trifecta of deliciousness!
New World option: Robert Modavi Moscato D' Oro 2013, Napa
Old World option: Castello del Poggio Moscato, Italy

Coconut Maple Granola with Peaches and Vanilla Ice Cream

Makes 4 cups

Who would've thought that a breakfast cereal would pair well with ice cream and dessert wine?! This homemade granola tastes delish as an ice cream topping or in a bowl with almond milk and a sliced banana on top!

---

2 cups rolled oats
1 cup raw nuts (I like almonds, pecans, and walnuts), roughly chopped
1/4 cup sweetened coconut flakes
2 Tbsp coconut sugar*
1/2 tsp cinnamon
Pinch sea salt (1/8 tsp)
1/3 cup pure maple syrup
3 Tbsp coconut oil
1/2 tsp pure vanilla extract

Organic White Peaches
Vanilla Ice Cream (dairy or non-dairy)

Preheat oven to 325°F. Combine oats, nuts, coconut, sugar, cinnamon, and salt in a large bowl. Heat coconut oil, maple syrup, and vanilla in the microwave for about 30-60 seconds, and mix until well blended. Immediately pour liquid ingredients into the oat mixture and stir until combined. Evenly spread granola on a large baking sheet.

Bake for 28-30 minutes, stirring once about halfway through baking time. The granola is done when golden brown and fragrant. Let cool completely before enjoying.

*Coconut sugar is a low-glycemic sweetener. If you don't have it, feel free to use brown sugar in this recipe.

Pairs best with: Sauternes
Exotic tropical fruit and honey give this wine a distinct flavor and undeniable ability to pair well with summer fruit and buttery pastry crusts.
Old World option: Chateau Miselle Sauternes 2016, France

How to Choose the Best Olive Oil

I am providing you with a quick reference guide on the standard olive oil categories and how to choose the best one for your specific needs.

Regular Olive Oil:
Labeled as "olive oil." You might find options like "light" or "robust," but it is definitely **not** extra virgin olive oil.
*This kind of olive oil is heavy enough for sautéing and roasting vegetables.
*Do not use this olive oil for bread dipping, salad dressings, or as a finish.

Extra Virgin Olive Oil (imported from Italy):
*Extra virgin olive oil is lighter in flavor and texture. You don't want to use this kind of olive oil for sautéing or roasting because the high heat will negatively impact the flavor.
*Imported extra virgin olive oil is better than regular olive oil for bread dipping, salad dressings, and as a finish.
*Most of the extra virgin olive oil on the store shelves in the United States comes from Italy or Spain. This might sound exotic, but it doesn't sound fresh!
Think how long it takes olive oil to be shipped to the grocery store and how long it sits on the store shelves under harsh lighting and varying temperatures.

Extra Virgin Olive Oil (local):
*This is by far the best route to go whenever extra virgin olive oil is called for in a dish.
*The price point for local extra virgin oil can be higher than the oil imported from Italy, but typically recipes that use extra virgin oil, need that specific flavor to really make the dish.

Avocado Oil (like you've seen in my recipes):
Avocado oil is a mild, multi-purpose olive oil that can be used for sautéing, roasting, and in salad dressings.

ACKNOWLEDGEMENTS

I want to first and foremost thank my husband David Nash; whose unconditional love and support created a space for me to follow my passions. Thank you to Dr. Tara Franks, who had faith in me as an author from the very beginning. Thanks to my graphic designer, Brianne Fortier, for creating such a beautiful book cover.

Thank you to my launch team Tiffany Hancock, Tara Franks, Natasha Jones, Brooke Lewis, David Nash, Elessia Bignall, and Cindy Deaver, who volunteered their time and support during the book launch. Thanks to editorial work provided by Kristen Forbes and Debra Kastner. Another big thanks to my cats Baxter and Dexter, for keeping me from going crazy while spending hours at home in front of the computer.

And last but certainly not least, I want to thank you for reading my book. The success of this book wouldn't be possible without your continued support.

Made in the USA
San Bernardino, CA
11 April 2019